199

The Cujo Cat Chronicles

To Jane & Zipper,
Kindest Regards & Headbonks!
Doug & Cujo
2-13-13

The Cujo Cat Chronicles

Musings of a Mad Housecat

Douglas Dunn/Cujo

To order additional copies of this book, contact:
Xlibris Corporation
1-888-795-4274
www.Xlibris.com
Orders@Xlibris.com
103609

Dedication

For My bride, Kathy. She is the reason for everything I do. To hear her giggle was the reason I started writing. Anyone who has ever heard the music of her giggle longs to hear it again. The world is a better place when she giggles.

Special thanks go out to all of Cujo's Facebook minions. Kelly Yorek, Susan Mayer, DeeDee Fabris (Lt.) Kirsha Wood, and all the other minions and MODS who encouraged me and spent so many evenings putting up with my warped sense of humor.

And finally, thank you to my Mom. Everyone who has ever met my Mom, has stated at one time or another that she was the origin of my wit.

Introduction

A couple of years ago, I was told about a website called: "The Owlbox". This was a website that streamed live video feed from a box that Carlos and Donna Royal had built atop a pole in their backyard. A pair of barn owls named Molly and Mcghee had taken up residence and had produced four gorgeous owlets. Watching Molly and Mcghee take care of their young ones was indeed special, however it paled in comparison with the magic that occurred on the Owlbox Social Stream.

From all over the world, people started talking to each other. We learned about one another. We shared jokes, wisdom, trials and troubles. We became deeply involved in supporting each other. We soon started calling ourselves "MODs" (Molly Obsessive Disorder). At any given hour, we could log on to the social stream and find someone to joke with, or a shoulder to cry on. This was one of the most special things that I have ever been involved with.

At some point each evening, I would share what my cat and resident tyrant, Raspittin, was up to, as well as what I thought might be going through his evil little mind. Soon, the other MODs nicknamed him "Cujo" and started encouraging me to write a blog based on his doings and philosophy. I decided "What the heck?" and figured I would post a dozen times or so and people would lose interest.

For reasons that escape me, the blog didn't die the expected quick and quiet death that I expected. I'm not sure who first suggested it, but at some point the MODs started recommending a book based on the blog. They have never steered me wrong, so with further encouragement from Cujo's fans, and of course the ever present foundation of my life, my bride Kathy, I took the leap.

What follows I owe all to them.

Just one other thing, No four leggers were harmed in the production of this book. However, several two leggers were traumatized both physically and mentally. The therapists say the voices should go away in a few years and in the meantime to ignore them when they tell me to do bad things.

In The Beginning

About a year ago, my two leggers talked me into starting a blog thingy. To tell the truth, I never thought that it would amount to much, nor last very long. One year later, I have discovered that the world has been hungering for truth, reason, honesty, wisdom and humility.

I have no idea where that can be found, but I suspect it may have been stolen by squirrels and hidden in some dark, dank hole in the middle of the squirrel homeland.

Probably in a tree.

I'd like to start by thanking all of my loyal minions. All of you have made this journey enjoyable and amusing. The comments that I have received have both shaped and influenced my ongoing philosophy. Though I may not reply to every comment, I assure you, I read and enjoy every one of them.

This last year, I have gotten to know and appreciate countless numbers of people across the world. I now have minions on every continent save Antartica, and I am currently working on networking with penguin thingies. On a daily basis, I chat with minions in 14 different time zones.

I find this absolutely amazing.

I also find in this an opportunity . . . .

This year I have spread my musings world wide. Now I plan to spread them further.

Oh sure, there are those who shall attempt to stop me. NASA has even canceled the shuttle program thingy in an effort to keep me earthbound. There is a movement in the Southeastern United States that worships squirrel thingies and wishes to see me overthrown. Their leader, the Right Honorable Nicholas McNuttjob, says I spread hate and discontent regarding his "flock".

Okay, I can't dispute that, but it is hurtful. If he and I ever meet in person, I will offer him an olive branch . . . . and then beat him about the head thingy with it.

Finally, please allow me to express my deepest appreciation for each and every one of you who take a few minutes from your busy day to read the musings of a tyrannical, smack happy housecat.

My Minions

First of all, I'd like to introduce my minions:

Doug—a creature of the hairless 2 legged variety. His activities consist of feeding me, buying me fuzzy toys that seem to amuse him more than me, and cleaning the royal litter.

Kathy—Doug's mate. She also feeds me and tells Doug to clean the royal litter.

Ivan the Tolerable—a fellow feline and my acting aide de camp. He is very large, easily mislead and quite dim. He is also my lead enforcer.

Tiger Lily—a female gray tabby. She's an accomplished whiner, but I keep her because she makes cool sounds when I smack her.

Now, a little about myself. The earth has been blessed with my presence for 3 1/2 years. I have been in charge of the Dunn family for most of that time. I have never had issues with humility. Humility is a vice I have chosen not to indulge in.

The Origin of The Cujo Dynasty

Lately, my two leggers have become somewhat nostalgic, telling stories about how they came to be graced with my presence. As usual, their stories have inaccuracies that portray the two leggers in a better light than they deserve.

If one was to hear the story of my "adoption" as they relay it, you would be led to believe that they rescued me from a dank, dark dungeon full of flea bitten prisoners with no chance of liberty. They found me, half starved, living off my own fur balls, sleeping on the cold, hard floor without even the bare comfort of a catnip mousie thingy.

Drivel.

I was born, the oldest kitten of eight, to an unwed female who lived with a single female two legger who spent a lot of time away from home. My mother was allowed to roam the neighborhood often, thus resulting in a midnight rendezvous that led to my glorious conception. Unable to support so many new dependants, I and my siblings were taken to the Vet's office where we were informed that we would be soon assigned new two leggers.

Subjected to a week long indoctrination process that involved a bath, several injections and humiliating examinations, we were instructed in how to behave in order to increase our chances of reassignment. Our instructor was an old tomcat that resided within the Vet's office named Reggie.

My first question was why, if Reggie was so good at this, hadn't he been reassigned?

But I digress.

During the indoctrination process, I decided that I would inflict more pain on the Vet and her assistants than they inflicted on me. In this endeavor, I was remarkably successful. I was placed in a large cage with fourteen other kittens to wait for my new two leggers. The other kittens were instructed to act "cute and adorable". Having known me for a week, Reggie simply asked me to refrain from bloodshed. I assured him I would try.

After spending several days watching two leggers come to the cage and select one kitten after another, I saw my opportunity. A male two legger approached the cage. I knew immediately that this was a two legger that could be easily tamed. He was tall, fairly thin with graying fur. Other than a clueless look in his eyes, what stood out most was the strange growth of fur between his upper lip and nose. It looked like he had tried to swallow a squirrel, but couldn't quite finish the job.

I immediately climbed to the top of the cage and stuck my paw through the wire successfully managing to sink a claw into his leg in order to gain his attention. I informed him that he was to look no further, his master was at hand. I ordered him to sign the paperwork and get me outta there.

He of course complied.

The relief among the staff at the veterinary clinic was evident. As word of my impending departure circulated through the office, gasps of joy and elation were heard. I suspect there may even have been dancing. The Vet quickly decided that as of the day of my adoption, a strict "No Returns" policy was to be implemented. I am unsure what this policy entails, but I got the feeling that I was credited with this change in policy. I heard later that it was called "The Cujo Clause".

He brought me into my new house in the "kitty carrier" thingy. Upon placing me on the floor, he opened the door on the kitty carrier and I entered my kingdom.

The first thing I beheld was a large, obviously mentally challenged orange tabby. Ivan at that time was approximately three times my size (I was only 12 weeks old) and twenty times my weight. I instantly decided that he would be my chief minion, so I poofed and promptly smacked him. Ivan fled down the hallway like a furry orange bowling ball, presumably to assure that the rest of my house would be properly prepared for me. My new house was full of toys and breakable stuff. After making a full examination, I informed the two legger that my new abode was acceptable.

About an hour later, the mate of the male two legger arrived. The male tried to warn her that the house had changed ownership, but she told him that he was exaggerating. She picked me up, cooing and stroking me in a very gentle manner. The male stood aghast as she petted the "sweet wittle putty cat". When he spoke of returning the "little hellbeast" to the place from whence it came, she told him that this was my home now.

Truer words never spoken.

Ivan The Tolerable

Let me give a description and short biography of this freak of nature: Ivan is a feline that seems to be created of spare parts. He has a tiny head mounted on a very large torso which is in turn mounted on extremely short stubby legs and followed by a short bottle brush tail. His markings are that of an orange tabby. Though his head is small, in comparison, his brain is like a BB in a boxcar. He is denser than a clump in a litter box.

Since he is the closest thing to a friend that I have ever chosen to have, I will not insult him. I have never understood why, but he speaks with a Brooklyn thug accent.

Ivan is nine months older than I, and approximately five pounds heavier. He is a complete neat freak.

I first met Ivan when the two leggers brought me to my new kingdom. His unnaturally small head was the first thing I saw as I exited the kitty carrier thingy. As I came out, I beheld the most perplexing sight.

Ivan.

His first reaction to me was to say "Ummmm hiss?"

I smacked the hiss outta him and proceeded to lay claim to the rest of my kingdom.

However, I continued to keep an eye on him. I quickly realized that Ivan does have some endearing qualities:

1. Being extraordinarily dim, he is easily manipulated.
2. Being extraordinarily dim, he is also incredibly loyal.
3. Being extraordinarily dim, he doesn't know when you are making fun of him.
4. Being extraordinarily dim, he fears nothing.
5. Being extraordinarily dim, he forgets to hold grudges.

Did I mention he's dim?

Ivan also has a very short fuse. Once, I observed him get so angry with his own paw that he refused to use it for ten minutes. It was amusing to watch him limp around on three legs.

For the most part, the two leggers are the recipients of Ivan's wrath. When Ivan is in a "mood", no ankle is safe. One can spot when he becomes perturbed. His sad excuse for a tail suddenly starts twitching like a conductors baton, his micro-mouth becomes locked in the open position and he stalks the room looking for something to place in his jaws.

He can chomp like no one I have ever seen. His chomp has been known to make rocks cry. His chomp is spoken of with reverence among shark thingies. There are pit bulls that are lobbying to have his chomp regulated.

On the other hand, when Ivan is happy, he is also quite amusing. When he feels frisky, he suddenly crooks his tail and with a trill, stampedes up and down the hallway making a sound not unlike an elephant thingy in heat. He bounces around like a fuzzy orange bowling ball leaving fear and destruction in his wake. Several earthquakes have been attributed to his shenanigans. Chaos follows him wherever he goes.

I love that about him.

Tiger Lily
(Queen of The Whine Country)

Tiger Lily is a five year old gray tabby. She is somewhat chubby and has an abnormally large face. Her most common expression is one of disdain.

Tiger Lily came to live in my house approximately two and a half years ago. This was **NOT** my idea.

Apparently one of my two legger's offspring felt that Tiger Lily needed a different home and sent her to me. Being the generous soul that everyone knows I am, I decided this was acceptable.

Immediately upon her arrival, I decided she needed a smack in order to establish that this was my house and that she lived here at my sufferance. This served its intended purpose, however, it had an added bonus.

It amused me.

Now I cannot speak for any of my readers, but I find that some individuals just give off some "I need a good smacking" vibe. Tiger Lily has this vibe on steroids. Just smelling her from across the room can start my paw twitching.

As if this vibe is not enough, she whines.

No, I mean she WHINES.

If her mouth is moving, she is either eating, sneezing or whining. I personally have witnessed her doing all three at once. Every time she whines while the two leggers are home, I get either sprayed with water, or at the very least, chastised.

This annoys me.

This is truly smack-worthy. I suspect that sometimes she whines just to get me in trouble. That's sneaky and underhanded, so I do have to give her some credit.

And it's not just me, Ivan enjoys smacking her as well. If she ventures into the bathroom, even the bathroom spider will take a swing. I'll lay money that if she ever finds herself outside, there would be a line of woodland creatures standing patiently in my yard awaiting their turn at her.

So please, don't blame me. It's not my fault. She is simply smackable.

And be warned, if I get one more e-mail accusing me of unwarranted smacking, I may feel compelled to go smack her.

Two Leggers

I do not detest two leggers. On the contrary, I love two leggers. I love the fact that they feed me. I love the fact that they clean my litter. I love them in the way that all benevolent dictators love their oppressed citizenry.

Two leggers have such potential. They are capable of creating great works of art, of composing beautiful music, of inventing such incredibly useful technology as the Chia Pet.

They spend much of their time inventing things to simplify their lives only to have those very inventions complicate their lives further.

They watch the talking box thingy to escape the reality of their lives. What do they watch on the talking box thingy? Yup, reality shows.

They teach their young to love one another and never raise a paw in anger. They then give them video game thingies in which the goal is to kill everyone in sight.

They'll spend hours on the computer thingy trying to get other two leggers on other computer thingies to be their "neighbors", but not wave to the two legger that lives next door.

No, I do not detest two leggers at all. They keep me amused.

Roots

During the course of writing my book thingy, I have received requests for more information about my two leggers. I know not why anyone would be interested in them, but being the ever congenial tyrant that I am, I have decided to comply.

So I present to you, Doug's family history as told by . . . . Doug.

"My ancestors originally arrived in this great land (America) in 1870. Twenty year-old Daniel Dunn arrived here from Ireland and immediately headed west to seek his fortune. Daniel found gainful employment with General Custer's 7th Cavalry as head poop picker upper. His job was to follow the cavalry and clear the trail so that the infantry would not get their feet dirty with the excrement of the preceding beasts of burden. Danny 'Greenboots' Dunn, as Custer liked to call him, served meritoriously until 1876 when the 7th Cavalry met its' fate at the Little Big Horn. Danny was not present at the battle, however he did arrive the next day and did his duty by clearing the battleground of all fecal matter. For this he was awarded the Brown Star of Valor and summarily discharged from the Army.

"Danny then went into private practice. In 1890, he became rich after inventing the Poop Limiting Undertail Gizmo (P.L.U.G. for short) However, the advent of the automobile and several unfortunate cases of exploding horses limited the success of his invention.

"In 1892, Danny met the love of his life, Doreen. Doreen was a former side show performer and recreational gypsy. She was fired from the side show after losing one of her three eyes in an unfortunate bratwurst making accident. The sideshow already had several two-eyed women and so she was laid off. Danny and Doreen settled in central Texas where they raised their two children, Poolina and Duke. Poolina passed away in infancy.

"Duke, under his loving parents guidance, grew into a strapping young man of 4'11". Nicknamed 'Duke', he left home at three years old to seek his fortune.

"Duke met his bride Eileen in 1952. Ironically, Eileen was a one legged waitress working at IHOP. She and Duke settled on the family farm where they made a living raising canned hams. They also tried raising lean beef, but the cows kept blowing away in the high Texas winds.

"In 1966, Eileen gave birth to me. Duke and Eileen raised me as if I was one of their own. The youngest of one, I was forced to wear my own hand me downs. It was rough country life. Our furniture was made of mud and cactus. I recall waiting by the horse stop, (our school was too poor to afford buses) in the middle of the harsh Texas winter. One year it actually got down to 60 degrees. But I never complained. Duke always told me "Remember son, that in other parts of the world, there are kids who are much smarter and handsomer than you". I'm not sure how that helped, but that was his way.

"In 1984, I joined the U.S. Navy. The Navy taught me how to wear shoes that tie and how to open a beer bottle with my teeth. I cannot understate how that experience changed my life.

"I was discharged in 1987 when it was discovered that that I had only one functioning nostril. At loose ends, I wandered around looking for a job wherein which I could cut, burn and mutilate myself and yet still get paid. Goldsmithing was the perfect fit."

The rest is history.

The Servitude of The Two Leggers

I have received numerous comments referring to my two leggers as being my "slaves". I take exception to this misnomer. I have never considered them to be my slaves. Please allow me to explain:

My male two legger spends much of his free time watching the talking box thingy. His favorite channel is probably the History Channel. Therefore, I have learned much of two legger history while gracing him with my presence.

Now as I understand it, slavery was something the two leggers practiced during the darker parts of their development. One group of two leggers found another group of two leggers and forced them to do their bidding. The group that subjugated the other group were known as the "masters". The subjugated were the "slaves". Obviously this was not an equally beneficial relationship.

Now, I can somewhat understand why one might consider yours truly to be a "master" and my two leggers my "slaves", but please consider this: Did the two legger slaves go to a shelter and look for the cutest master to take home? Have you ever heard of a cat chasing down a runaway two legger?

I prefer to think of my two leggers as minions. While I am of course the supreme ruler of my dominion, rather than a state of slavery, I consider it to be more of a benevolent dictatorship. They provide me with all that I need: Food, places to sleep, litter box service, catnip mousie thingies . . . . etc. In return, I bless them with my presence. I warm their laps. I slay their dust bunnies and scowl at their squirrels. I even take the time to smack any whiny pets they may adopt.

This is a mutually beneficial relationship. They are not my slaves, they are my thralls.

Now, that being said, like any good dictator, I must rule with an iron paw. When the two leggers act up, they must be punished. The severity of punishment varies with the seriousness of the transgression. Anything from a snubbing to complete designer shoe destruction. If I am too busy, or just disinterested, I send Ivan to administer justice. The only problem with relegating this duty to Ivan is that he can occasionally be a bit over-enthusiastic in his judicial endeavors. Luckily, my two leggers have learned their lesson and now keep a copious supply of band aid thingies.

In Your Facebook

I have been observing the two leggers. I am confused. While two legger behavior is often confusing, it is seldom book worthy. In this case, I feel I must reach out to my readers and ask them to explain this particular oddness.

The oddness I refer to is called "Facebook". At first glance, Facebook, or "FB" as the oddest two leggers call it, seemed to be a way for two leggers who live in different areas to communicate with each other. I can see the reasoning behind this. I myself wouldn't mind contacting my old littermates and bragging about how I conquered and developed my kingdom. This would be amusing. I would share my wisdom and catnip procurement strategies. Perhaps I would even "franchise" my kingdom. Imagine a world where there was a Cujoish cat in every home that had internet access. Truly a utopian society.

Back to the two leggers. Do they use this technology in the noble pursuit of spreading Cujoness everywhere? No. They use it to tell each other what they had for dinner. They tell each other every single thing that they "like". They show each other silly picture thingies. But most of all, they play games in which they do things that in real life they consider chores.

Take "Farmville". I have observed my male two legger spending hours planting and harvesting crops, feeding and combing animals, building fences and barns. Meanwhile, my lawn needs mowing, I am hungry, my fur is matted, and my roof leaks. Maybe if I awarded useless imaginary money for taking care of us, I'd never again have to witness Ivan sulking because he can see the bottom of his food bowl.

One other thing that annoys me about Facebook is that they have a "like" button thingy. Why only "like"? If I was in charge there would be several more button thingies:

Annoy
Amuse
Smack
Snub
Smack Again

They do have an "ignore" button, but by pressing it aren't you actually "paying attention"?

So please, if you can enlighten me, do so.

Family Time

Ugh.

My two leggers have recently mandated a new type of Hell. They call it "family time".

Ever since their offspring escaped, the two leggers have now unleashed their un-pasteurized affection upon myself and my four legged minions. Adoration, admiration and worshipful awe are welcomed and of course, expected, but affection is unacceptable.

Affection is an emotion that implies the expectation of the return of the same emotion. Silly two leggers. When will they learn?

Anyway, I digress. Family time occurs every evening at ten o'clock sharp. The two leggers retire to their bed in order to watch the talking box thingy and expect us feline types to join them. They even go so far as to pick us up and lock us in the bedroom. As if we don't have better things to do. There are dust bunnies to harvest and "knock-knacks" (not a typo) to "rearrange". These are things that are difficult to accomplish while the two leggers are up and about.

We have learned to accept this daily purgatory, though we refuse to like it.

Tiger Lily curls up on the pillow behind the female's head, usually with her tail tickling the female's ear. This amuses her. Ivan sprawls with his ample weight equally distributed across both the two leggers raising their body temperature by an average of 115 degrees Fahrenheit. I meanwhile, am not so predictable. Sometimes I curl up and pretend to nap on the end of the bed, but not often. I prefer activities that cause more mayhem.

For instance, I have found that by sitting on top of the talking box thingy and giving the two leggers my patented "owl-face" glare, I can irritate them to the point that they end up letting me out. It also amuses me to walk along the bedstands enforcing the law of gravity on anything that may be pushed off.

But what amuses me the most is sneaking along the side of the bed, waiting until I am precisely even with Tiger Lily's position, and then leaping upon her without warning. This invariably causes a chain reaction of chaos. Startling Tiger Lily causes her to poof, jump and declare her displeasure in an incredibly loud whine (not always in that order). This startles both two leggers which in turn causes Ivan to poof and fly off the bed and run into the nearest wall. Pictures have been known to be knocked down by Ivan's impact with the wall. This never fails to make the two leggers so frustrated that me and my cohorts are declared unfit for family time and banished from the bedroom.

Mission accomplished.

Love and Other Nasty Habits

Now, of all the two legged behaviors I do not pretend to understand, my two leggers mating rituals top the list. They seem to be in constant physical contact with each other, holding hands, touching lips . . . etc . . . .

I have spent many hours watching the talking box thingy and from what I have gathered, these are not the normal actions of a mated pair of two leggers that have been paired as long as mine have.

According to the talking box thingy, two legger relationships follow a very common chronological order:

1. They meet, and after establishing common interest, they begin sharing meals.
2. They share more meals and then decide to share their meals exclusively with one another.
3. They decide to share a house together. (generally without consulting the reigning four legger in residence)
4. After sharing their home for a few years, they begin to tire of each other's presence and insult each other incessantly.
5. At some point during their relationship, they breed and produce offspring that are smart mouthed and irritating. These offspring are usually arrested later and go into something called "rehab".
6. Some kid named "Timmy" falls into a well thingy and a dog tricks the two leggers into saving him.
7. The two leggers eventually grow old and disenchanted with one another until the show is canceled.

My two leggers seem to ignore these rules.

They can't seem to get past stage 3.

I keep trying to tell them to move on. They are interrupting the natural order of things. By now, they should be yelling at each other on a daily basis. Yet in the four years I have been observing them, I have never witnessed a moment of non feline induced anger between them. They have never raised their voices, insulted or spouted venom at each other. Not once has the male slept in the living room. Never have I witnessed a single instance of discord.

In fact, truth be known, they have only grown closer with time.

Now, if things weren't bad enough, we are rapidly approaching the two legger holiday that celebrates love and affection. They call it "Valentine's Day".

I cannot over stress my annoyance.

It gets worse.

Exactly one month after this holiday, my two leggers celebrate the day that annually marks the day that they were mated.

Please, if you are capable, send help. I may not survive all this mooshiness. Somewhere there must be an animal cruelty law that prohibits two leggers from exposing their resident four leggers to such sickening behavior.

I can tell that the next few weeks are gonna put extreme stress on my catnip reservoir. I may have to dip into Ivan's.

Think I'll go wish Tiger Lily a Slappy Valentine's Day.

Another Mystery Solved

The two legger belonging to Dandi Butt and Tony T once wrote me and asked me to inform them why two leggers insist on smearing icky sticky stinky stuff beneath their arms. As an avid observer of two legger behavior, I am profoundly capable of answering this.

Two leggers are both ashamed and afraid of their own scent. We four legged types are extremely proud of our individual scents. They serve many purposes. Our scent is our message to other creatures. It says "Here I am, deal with it!". Or "I was here and now that I have touched this, it belongs to me". It can also mean "Dogs not tolerated". Our scent is our personal calling card. We are proud of it and utilize every method at our disposal to spread it as far and wide as possible.

Two leggers on the other hand, seek to hide or disguise their scent at every opportunity. They actually prefer to smell like the people on the talking box thingy. Now I must admit that I have yet to smell a pleasant smelling two legger, (except that tuna fisherman that came over for dinner) however, most of them still smell better than Ivan. So they seek to cover their scent by rubbing stinky gooey sticks on their bodies.

The best way to tell that a two legger has been in your stuff is that it smells distinctly unlike a two legger.

I trust that once again my wisdom has enlightened all.

Ghost Hunters (Home Edition)

It is the "wee hours" of the night.

I know this because the female two legger just got up and went "wee".

Normally this time of night is very quiet. It is usually the time of darkness during which Ivan and I plot our activities and chaos for the coming day. Tiger Lily is locked in the computer room and unavailable for therapeutic smacking. The two leggers are sleeping soundly in their bed completely unaware of our plotting.

Ivan and I continue to plot. It is becoming increasingly difficult to come up with new forms of mischief. For every action there is an equal and opposite reaction. We cause chaos, they attempt to restore order into their little world. However, I am confident that chaos will always triumph.

As we sit in the living room plotting, our ears are beset by a most eerie sound. Mere words fail to describe it. If I heard this sound emanating from the talking box thingy while it was tuned to the Sci-fi channel, college students would be running for their lives while an alcoholic priest suddenly finds his true calling again and rushes into the house to exercise the spirit. Why spirits need exercise is beyond me, must be a Richard Simmons thingy, but I digress.

This sound reverberates throughout my house like all the demons of the netherworld trying to once again take over New York. (I am not convinced they have ever been vanquished from New York, but once again, I digress)

If you have ever watched "Ax-Men" on the talking box thingy, and if you have ever heard "Rap" music, take the sounds from those two things, add the sound of a lawn mower thingy, throw in a tuba and a poorly tuned violin, add a teaspoon of Celine Dion and a pinch of "American Idol" tryouts, and you have a small example of the noise.

What can this horrid sound possibly be?

I turn to Ivan seeking his counsel. This to no avail, given that Ivan has been reduced to a quivering puddle of orange dumbdom. He is in the process of imitating a striped peach and apricot Jello mold gone horribly wrong.

As usual, it falls to me to seek out and vanquish the foe. I am not saying that I am the John Wayne of feline society, Ok, maybe I am saying that, but when I confront a mystery, my feline instincts shift to high gear until the mystery is both solved and turned to my advantage.

The sound seems to be emanating from the back of my house. This is where I allow the two leggers to sleep. They call it the "bedroom", I call it the . . . well, bedroom. It is where the bed is, so, though unoriginal, bedroom it is.

I approach the bedroom on full alert. Smack first, and second, and smack a third time before I ask questions is my philosophy. In short order, I realize that this Hell begotten sound is not emanating from a curio that the two leggers brought home from another flea market. (These flea markets feature Gypsies and other sordid folk, which they enjoy visiting on weekends because it makes them feel "artsy".) It is coming from the male two legger's face.

At first glance, I am unable to comprehend what I am seeing. Surely my mild mannered two legger could not be capable of producing such a cacophony of audio torture.

I must test my hypothesis.

Using my entire weekly ration of stealth, I climb upon the bed. Careful not to wake the two leggers, I walk to the to top of the bed covers and observe. The male is sleeping with his mouth wide open and emitting the offending sounds. Very carefully, I place both paws into his mouth effectively cutting off his respiratory passages.

The noise ceases.

I remove my paws.

The noise returns.

I once again place my paws in his mouth.

The noise again ceases.

Mystery solved.

I go back and inform Ivan that I have forced the evil spirit from our house. I also mention that the only way to keep the vanquished from returning, is by giving the vanquisher half of his food from now on.

This will serve the greater good. I will be even more well fed and Ivan will lose some of that gut.

As for the two legger, he is still wondering why he wakes every morning with cat hair on his tongue.

Some mysteries are better left unexplained.

Snot Funny

My male two legger has undergone a transformation.

A transformation of both mind and body.

I am very amused.

It began Tuesday.

Tuesday began much like any other day in my world. The two leggers woke up, fed Ivan and Tiger Lily, and gave me my morning worship. They then showered, drank coffee, and left to go wherever it is they go on Tuesday.

The first sign that anything was amiss came that evening when they arrived home. The male was even paler than his normal coloration. When he spoke, it sounded like a cross between a duck and a lawnmower.

But most disturbing of all was the substance that oozed from his face. It appeared to be the same substance that snail thingies leave in their wake when they cross my deck. After much pondering, I came to the conclusion that he had spent the day shoving snails up his nose and was now paying the price for such an ill considered decision.

After watching him for the remainder of the evening, I decided that my first hypothesis was incorrect. Given his somewhat limited cranial capacity, there is no possible way that he could have fit that many snails into such a small space.

Further investigation was warranted. I stole one of the tissue thingies that he used in his attempts to stop the flow of the substance in question. It was damp, a bit slimy, and according to Ivan (my official taste tester) it tasted like chicken. I decided to call it "s'not". Owing to the fact that it's not liquid, and it's not solid either. Hence: "s'not".

Now, being a fan of gravity, (gravity is utilized by all felines world wide as part of our chaos inducing repertoire) I understand that the s'not could only be coming from the upper six inches of the two leggers head. His eyes did not show signs of deflation, so the only conclusion to be drawn is that the s'not is actually brain matter.

This makes sense. Since he started leaking, his thought processes have slowed. He seems very lethargic. He is almost unresponsive at times. Ivan enjoys this. He has a lap to inhabit all day and the two legger keeps forgetting that he's already been fed.

The only thing that puzzles me is the amount that is leaking. I would never have dreamed that he had that much to leak. I only hope it ceases before he lapses into a permanent vegetative state. If he should become comatose, I fear that he will no longer be to able clean the royal litter.

Tonight, while all is quiet, I will hold his nose open while Ivan stuffs the tissue thingies back up into his head.

We can save him.

Two Legger Younglings

I have often pondered the spawn of the two leggers.

They appear to be miniature versions of their parents, but that is where the similarities end.

They eat much more and more often than their elders. They listen to obnoxious music. They abhor bathing and hygiene on principle. Their clothing is ludicrous at best.

However, I must in all honesty admit that they have some qualities that are to be commended. Sneaky and underhanded in the extreme, they will stoop to any level to get their way. I respect that. Their rooms smell worse than most litter boxes and contain nastier nuggets. They constantly strive to find new and innovative ways to distress their adult two leggers. I have witnessed this on numerous occasions and it never fails to amuse me.

The sphere of chaos that seems to orbit the adolescent two legger is a sight to behold. Things breaking, mature two leggers screaming, Tiger Lily poofed, It is awe-inspiring to see a master at work.

Fortunately, there are no offspring in permanent residence in my abode. My two leggers have raised their litter and found suitable homes for them. I'm not sure if they took them to the shelter or found homes for them, but they occasionally visit, though they seem to have grown out of their damage causing years.

Recently, some of the litter returned:

They arrived, entering my abode in the middle of my early-mid afternoon nap. They came bearing luggage, not food. Their luggage smelled of other felines which I found interesting, but annoying. I immediately decided that the bags now belonged to me and set forth in an effort to eradicate the offending scents.

I will now describe the invaders. The female offspring is called "Erica". She has the same coloring as her mother, but tends to display her teeth more often than is generally acceptable. (Though not in a hostile manner). I have noticed that in two legger culture this dental display is a sign of contentment or even "happiness".

Truly annoying.

Her mate "Kelly", embodies a trait that I find pleasing in a two legger: He rarely speaks at all. Though he appears "happy" as well, this quietude makes up for this "happiness".

I was to learn later that this "happiness" stemmed from the fact that on Christmas Day, they became "engaged". Apparently, when two leggers find someone that they are compatible with, they decide to commit themselves to one mate for the rest of their lives. This in turn makes them and all their two legged family members "happy".

I don't get it either.

Now, I have known Erica since I was a kitten and have always considered her to be a sort of long distance minion. Or perhaps a minion by birth. I'm not sure which is more applicable, but suffice it to say she is a minion. She comes to my home once or twice a year presumably to see me, and possibly visit my two leggers while she is here. Her adoration of me is acceptable if somewhat unpracticed.

Her new-found mate I have only met once before. He seems to have some dog loving traits, but I believe that given time, this can be corrected. As he entered my house, I inspected him and after some preemptive petting and scratching behind my ears, he settled onto my couch and provided a lap. I found this courteous and accepted his offering.

I decided that he had reached the level of Probationary Minion.

Ivan and Tiger Lily showed less discretion and accepted him instantly.

The only friction between us and the two leggers came when Erica realized that Ivan would nap on every two legger lap, save hers. There is a simple explanation for this. Erica's lap contains no padding. Ivan needs padding. A simple pillow would have solved this misunderstanding.

Well, Erica and Kelly left today to return to someplace the two leggers call the "air force". This confuses me because the only "air force" that I am aware of originates below Ivan's tail. This bears pondering.

Baby Stalk

I once received a message from one of my four legged followers begging me to advise her on dealing with an interloper recently introduced to her household. This fresh irritant is referred to by the two leggers as a "baby". Having once seen one, I feel imminently qualified to advise her. The message reads:

"Dear Great, Wise, Wonderful, Fantastic, Handsome, Brilliant, Ingenious, and Famous Cujo Cat,

"I have a problem that requires your sage counsel. My female two legger recently underwent an inexplicable nine month long weight gain. During this time she became quite unpredictable in both her general disposition as well as her appetite. This also affected the male two legger causing him to take a sudden interest in building stuff. He even went as far as to evict me from my favorite dayroom and re-paint it a nasty shade of pink. He replaced my kitty condo with a miniature two legger bed that has bars on the side.

"Then one day there was chaos, and not the good, feline induced type. The two leggers left in the middle of the night and did not return for two days. The only two legger I saw during this time was the male's sibling that came briefly to fill my food and water.

"On the third day, the two leggers returned carrying a bundle of screaming rags. Since then, there has been little peace and less affection shown to Yours Truly. The screaming rags turned out to be a "baby". I don't understand what could possess my two leggers to bring this into my domicile, let alone why they continue to feed it. I await your wisdom.

"Thank you,
Minnie Mousemunch"

I replied:

"Dear Minnie,

First of all, your salutation (Dear Great, Wise, Wonderful, Fantastic, Handsome, Brilliant, Ingenious, and Famous Cujo Cat,) is flattering, but overdone. (I'm not that famous)

"I understand your dilemma. These "baby" thingies are truly a bane to all cats everywhere. After doing some research and observation, I have reached the conclusion that they are embryonic two leggers. I believe that the nine month period of weight gain that you witnessed was actually the female's pregnancy. When they disappeared for two days, they probably went to the Vet for the delivery. I do find it curious however that they only brought one of the litter home with them. Perhaps they were offered their pick and this was the one they chose.

"Be that as it may, I feel that the best course of action is to observe, plot and whenever possible, wreak havoc. I suggest you act as though you enjoy the company of the embryo. Purr when it is called for, but don't lay it on too thick. If you are too nice, the two leggers will suspect your motives.

"Be wary of their defense mechanisms. They have the ability to emit a stench that even Ivan cannot abide. Their vocalizations can actually cause glass to break and milk to sour.

So tread carefully. As for the bars around the miniature bed, I think they are there in order to keep the "baby" from sneaking out and murdering them in their sleep. (I actually saw that happen on the talking box thingy once)

"There is one benefit to having one of these in your household however. Whenever you are left alone with the "baby", you have carte blanche to break stuff. The mature two leggers will just smile at the "baby" and call it a 'little rascal" or some such drivel. I know it's not fair (they should spray it with the squirty water thingy) but when it's their offspring, it suddenly seems cute to them. So enjoy the freedom to break anything you want without consequence. Just make sure it lands near the "baby".

"Finally, if it gets to be too much for you to handle, c'mon over to my place. We'll do some nip and slap Tiger Lily. It's very therapeutic.""

Litter Laws

I find myself in the unenviable state of confusion.

There has been much chaos and upheaval within my kingdom of late.

As a rule, I generally enjoy chaos and upheaval. However, this chaos and upheaval has not been of my creation. Therefore it annoys and confuses me.

From what I have been able to gather, one of my two legger's offspring had been bred last year and was expecting to give birth. Why this is such a cause for both concern and joy among the two leggers is beyond me.

Two leggers seem to dote on their progeny. No, "dote" is understating the case. They obsess over their progeny. Even after their offspring have moved out or been sent to a shelter, they concern themselves with all the whereabouts and activities of their young. They worry incessantly over the choices that they are making.

Troubled by the thought of a third generation of my two legger's being brought into existence, I have pondered much these last two days. I have drawn some conclusions.

First of all, I believe that two leggers obsess over their young because their litters are so small. They usually bear only one at a time. Occasionally two and on rare occasions three. (If a two legger gives birth to more than three at once, they are required to have a talking box thingy program made about them.)

Two legger offspring also grow at an incredibly slow pace. I consider this to be a sign of recessed evolution. They do not even begin to wean until they are nearly a year old. In fact, there are a lot of things that they start doing only after a full year of development.

Walking
Talking
Using the litter box without assistance.

However, to give the newborn two leggers credit, there are several things that they seem to know instinctively from birth:

> Gurgling
> Slobbering
> Sticking things (fingers as well as foreign objects) into their noses.
> Plus, they have the most amazing capacity for creating odors that puts even Ivan to shame.

They are totally dependent on their parents for at least the first ten years of their lives. In many cases they remain dependent on them until well into their thirties.

As in all things, the two leggers should learn from their feline betters:

> The first week after birth, teach your young to walk.
> Wean them at twelve weeks.
> Kick them out at six months.
> Have more than one litter per year.

And above all, have larger litters. That way when one turns out odd or touched in the head, you've got some "normal" ones to continue your bloodline.

The Devil in The De-Tails

Once again, my house has been invaded.

This time it has been invaded by another two legger.

She is another offspring of the resident two leggers.

She is the youngest female of the brood.

She showers me with gifts and adoration.

She is called The Stephanie.

I find The Stephanie interesting. Though she is a two legger, she is also a four wheeler. It would seem that she has decided that walking is too "pedestrian" for her. So she sits upon her wheely thingy and moves through my house at twice the speed of Ivan. (approximately .75 mph)

The wheely thingy runs over or plows through every obstacle it encounters. This is worthy of my respect. That being said, it also happens to be the arch enemy of long tailed felines everywhere. The wheely thingy lies in wait until it spots an unattended tail, and then it strikes. Rolling out of nowhere, it attempts to run over said tail causing the owner of the aforementioned tail to howl in pain and bewilderment. Generally, this triggers a mass feline exodus from the room and much chaos ensues.

You would think that such a potential for damage and havoc would please and amuse me.

In this case, you would be wrong.

If you recall, I mentioned that the wheely thingy feeds on LONG cat tails. Given the fact that I have the longest tail in my kingdom, I am its' favorite prey. Ivan has nothing to worry about. His tail is even shorter than his longest train of thought. Tiger Lily is safe because I smacked her tail clean off several weeks ago.

So that leaves me. I refuse to be defeated. I have a plan.

Every night, The Stephanie leaves the wheely thingy in the living room. It appears to go dormant whenever she leaves it alone. So tonight while it sleeps, Ivan and I plan to give it a smacking it will never forget.

When it wakes in the morning, bruised, battered and covered in semi digested hairballs, it will know . . . .

You don't mess with The Paw.

The Gathering

I have on occasion observed a phenomenon where suddenly a large group of two leggers show up at my house and stay for several hours.

This does not amuse me.

I do not know how they know that at a particular hour, on a particular evening, my two leggers will suddenly discover a surplus of food and beverages, but through some strange two legger instinct they just seem to show up. It is perplexing.

Granted these gatherings aren't completely without their precursors. Usually on the morning of the gathering, the two leggers will rise early and begin a manic scrubbing of every surface in my home. They round up all the dust bunnies. They break out that bane of feline existence, the hoover sucky thingy and proceed to gather all the hair that has taken weeks for me to place in an esthetically pleasing arrangement. They scoop the royal litter. They even scrub their own water filled litter box, even though they may have cleaned it only two months previously.

By mid-afternoon, the male two legger begins to make multiple trips to the backyard where he makes a fire and starts turning perfectly good meat into hard, blackened bricks that he takes great pride in showing to the other males when they arrive. Perhaps the ability to make soft pink things into hard black things is a great feat in two legger society.

I don't understand.

Generally within an hour of the ceremonial flames being lit, the other two leggers descend upon my residence like a plague of locusts that travel in swarms of two. They show absolutely no respect to the four legged rulers of the household. When they notice me at all, they usually say such insulting things as: "Ooh, look at the cute little kitty" or "Oh! how sweet, he's smiling at me!"

Ok, that "smile" is actually my method of displaying that my teeth are longer and sharper than theirs, and I guarantee much more experienced at dealing with annoyances.

The definition of an "annoyance" is anyone referring to me as "a cute little kitty".

If the gathering occurs during cold or wet weather, I can usually exact some form of vengeance due to the fact that the two leggers often remove their shoes at the door, and place their coats on the bed in the spare room. This allows Ivan and I to strategically distribute a ration of hairball thingies in the shoes, while Tiger Lily wallows on their coats covering them liberally with gray mats of fur. Though she is a whiny, sneezing, fun to smack type of fellow feline, she can shed like nobody's business.

The only positive about these gatherings, is that invariably, my two leggers will afterwards decide that they are too tired to clean and go to bed. Thus begins the midnight buffet which will continue until Ivan passes out on the kitchen floor and Tiger Lily tattles to the two leggers.

The Gathering Part II

It is six months later and we are NOT amused.

I am not speaking of the "Royal We", I am speaking of the four legged denizens of my kingdom. From myself, right down the slapping order to Tiger Lily.

As a matter of fact, we have been pushed beyond "not amused". We have been driven past Annoyedville and are within spitting distance of Pissedburgh.

The two leggers have surpassed themselves in the area of insubordination. Allow me to explain:

First of all, let's jump into our "way back machine thingy" and go back to last Thursday.

Thursday is one of the days that the two leggers do not wake up and go to work. Sometimes, they hardly wake at all on Thursday. But on this particular Thursday, they woke up early and commenced to scrubbing everything in sight. They dusted, cleaned the kitchen, and corralled every dust bunny they could find. They even found some of their possessions that I had carefully concealed in my numerous hidey holes. This furious activity aroused my curiosity, but had not crossed the line at which I become annoyed.

Having observed all this, the realization suddenly struck me. The two leggers were planning a gathering.

It is not often that my two leggers host a gathering. Frankly, I am not sure why two leggers gather in the first place. When they gather, they usually eat, drink things that make them act doglike and then they sit around and talk. There is no hissing. No poofing or raising of hackles. Blood is seldom shed, and there is very little smacking involved. The purpose of theses gatherings escapes me.

Having surmised the reason for the all the cleaning, I immediately called Ivan and Tiger Lily into a council of chaos plotting.

I ordered Ivan to conserve his gaseous emissions. I told him to save it all for a single gargantuan blast to be released seconds prior to the main course of the two leggers' dinner. I also gave him the duty of shredding any decorations the two leggers may put up in advance.

I gave Tiger Lily the responsibility of providing the "Whine du Jour". I told her she should practice her whining between the hours of two and five AM. so as to determine which vintage would cause the most desirable response. Tiger Lily has no claw thingies and is totally useless when it comes to physical destruction. I smacked her for this shortcoming and sent her to her room to ponder her lack of weaponry.

As for myself, I began working up the largest, nastiest, and slimiest hairball imaginable. This, I planned to release in a most dramatic fashion during dessert. This would be a true masterpiece of gastric recollection.

Friday came and the hectic preparations (two legged as well as four legged) continued. My lawn was mowed, my back deck swept, and all manner of things prepared. Ivan and I did our best to interfere, but since the preparations had moved outside, our efforts were limited at best.

On Saturday, the two leggers began to cook. We knew the day was at hand. We practiced our timing, and perfected our plan. We had retained much of the fur we would have shed earlier in order to deposit it on the coats of the two legged guests.

Everything was in readiness.

We waited in anticipation.

A car thingy approached my house.

And suddenly it happened. In an obviously pre-planned strategic maneuver, the two leggers grabbed us and tossed us unceremoniously into the spare bedroom. They told us it was "for our own good", but I doubt their veracity.

Ivan scratched at the door, I threatened them vehemently and questioned their pedigree. Finally finding a good use for Tiger Lily, I repeatedly slapped her against the window, almost managing to crack one pane. But it was to no avail. We suffered our banishment while the two leggers enjoyed their feast.

We were finally released only after the last two leggers had departed.

My two leggers feel smug now. They believe they have won. They are convinced that all is well.

They are mistaken.

I still have a hairball that has their new comforters' name written in big bold letters across it.

And let us not forget Ivan. Eventually he is going to explode, or shoot through the house like a released balloon thingy.

That should amuse me.

The Two Legger Litter Box

One of the questions I am most commonly asked is: "What's the deal with cats and bathrooms?"

The answer to this mystery is actually quite complex.

The first thing to consider is our aversion to closed doors. Given the fact that the bathroom door is the one door in the house that is almost always closed, we as cats see it as our duty and obligation to see that it is opened as often as possible.

The bathroom is invariably the warmest room in the house. enough said.

The next consideration is our sheer curiosity. The bathroom is an enigma to us felines. Two leggers use the bathroom for a myriad of reasons. Aside from it's use as a large self—cleaning litter box, it is also used for grooming, bathing and reading. This shows a clear lack of sophistication. No self respecting cat would ever groom itself while remaining in its own litter box. Reading and cleaning there is also out of the question.

I also observe the two leggers deliberately spraying water on themselves each and every morning. This behavior is truly confusing to me. When I act in a manner that displeases them, the two leggers spray me with water. Yet every morning they stumble half asleep to the bathroom and spray themselves.

You see my dilemma.

Perhaps the main reason we insist on being present in the bathroom, is that the irritation this causes provides us much amusement. That is why we wait exactly 45 seconds after door closure before we demand entry. This 45 second grace period enables the two legger in question to become fully seated on the self cleaning litter box. The amusement this causes cannot be measured. If the water spraying thingie is turned on, it is good to wait an additional two minutes for maximum effect.

The bathroom is also the ideal place to incarcerate an eight legger. It is usually the least furnished room in the kingdom. This makes it easier to keep an eye on the eight leggers given that there are fewer hidey holes in which it may lurk. But the best benefit it provides is that the two leggers are more easily creeped out by eight leggers when they are in a semi-clothed state. Keeping a spider thingy in the bathroom provides much amusement as well as a tasty snack in case one gets the munchies.

Sheet Happens

There is a subject that I would like to now address.

An obvious two legger wrote and asked me: "Why does my cat always have to get involved when I am trying to make my bed?"

First of all there are two misconceptions right off the bat. "Your cat?" "Your bed?"

Silly two legger.

There is a well known federal law that states: "If any bed in any household that is inhabited by a cat is in the process of being re-made, aforementioned cat must be allowed to supervise the making of aforementioned bed. This supervision may include, but is not limited to, such activities as:

1) Pouncing upon all sheets in a playful manner.
2) Crawling under the sheets thereby making it impossible for the sheets to lay flat.
3) Hooking a single claw in the sheet causing multiple snags.
4) Rolling on back and looking cute and innocent whilst you scream in joy.
5) Spreading enough cat hair to cover 4 cats on as much clean linen as possible.

Basically, any activity that retards the progress of the bed being made must be implemented. The spreading of the bottom (or fitted) sheet is an ideal opportunity for an enterprising feline to cause much aggravation on the part of the two leggers involved. This sheet is by design, almost impossible to fit over the mattress thingy. I am not sure why they call it a "fitted" sheet, unless it is due to the fact that the two leggers invariably pitch a "fit" before they are successful.

After the bed is successfully made, the two leggers will stand back, look at their wrinkleless handiwork, and congratulate themselves on a job well done. I allow them a five second grace period before pouncing upon the bed and proving once again that all two legger work is only temporary at best.

The laws of dignity are suspended while acting in this supervisory role.

Do not blame or yell at us, we are simply upholding the law.

This Old Cat House

Once again I have failed in my efforts to understand the two leggers.

The female of the species spends much of her leisure time watching the talking box thingy. Most of the people on the talking box thingy are telling her how to redecorate my house. She then tells the male two legger to leave and return with things that will apparently make my house look like the house on the talking box thingy. Confused? It gets better.

Everything the male returns with is spotless. No scratches. No threads out of place. No stains. Now after having watched this very same talking box thingy from my vantage point on the lap of the female, I have seen that the preferred condition of these things should be "distressed". Something about shabby being chic. I know nothing about shabby, (unless Ivan can be counted) but if there is one thing I do know, it is distressed. I consider myself an expert on causing both stress and distress. Therefore I see it as my duty to provide my professional touch to the aforementioned furnishings.

This generally causes the female to stamp her feet and shout with joy.

However, just as I get the furnishings to the proper level of distress, the female sends the male away from the house and he returns once again with all new stuff.

Many of the items that the male returns with require assembly after removal from the box. This provides much opportunity for chaos causing activity. One of my favorite activities involves the confiscation of unattended screw thingies. While the two legger is busily reading the unstructions (no typo) for the erection of the furniture, a simple swat will send a number of the screw thingies skittering across the carpet to the nether regions below the couch. Once beneath the couch, the screw thingies have entered a zone from which nothing has ever been recovered. It would seem that gravity is multiplied by a force of ten in the vicinity of the couch.

This also explains why on Sunday afternoons, the male's hindquarters get stuck on the couch whenever there is a football game on the talking box thingy.

The unstruction sheets themselves may provide amusement as well. Upon removal of the sheet, the two legger will spend the first five minutes trying to remember which language he is able to read. Once he is able to figure out which side of the sheet to read, he will read them several times. The unstructions are required to be written by first year law students who are trying to impress their professors with their knowledge of large nonsensical words. I can always measure the amount of his frustration by the movement of his lips while reading the unstructions. Generally speaking, the two legger will read the unstructions from start to finish about five times before yelling: "Screw this! I'm just gonna use the pictures!"

Using this method of furniture construction, the two legger will now assemble the entire unit. After completion, the female will enter the room and tell him that it is incorrect. He will then take the entire thing apart, and reassemble it once again. This time the female will enter the room and inform him that it is still incorrect, but it is incorrect in an entirely different way. After the fifth repetition of this ritual, she will pronounce that it is "good enough".

Once the furniture is deemed "good enough", the male then burns the unstructions in the firebox thingy and hides the screw thingies that were, for some odd reason, not needed.

Home of The Plopper

I am a world class plopper. For those who are unfamiliar with the term "plop" as it applies to feline activities, allow me to explain:

Plopping is something all cats do to some degree. It comes as naturally to us as purring or spider thumping. Plopping is basically defined as the act of suddenly appearing to lose all feeling in ones legs and thereby dropping to the floor in a boneless furry heap. There is no particular reason for us to do this, it simply amuses us.

There are several different styles of plopping. Ivan prefers the "Stop, Drop and Roll" method. This method is especially effective if used as a way to trip two leggers who happen to be walking in a darkened hallway. The purpose of the "roll" maneuver is that by rolling immediately to his back after the plop, Ivan instantly transforms from a soft pudgy cat into a totally immovable obstacle. He definitely gets credit for causing havoc, but loses points for style.

Tiger Lily often employs the "This Little Kitty Went wah wah wah All The Way Home" plop. This not truly a plop, it's more like her sitting on the floor whining, but I felt I should mention it.

My favorite plop is one I like to call the "Holey Sheet" technique. This is best done on the two leggers bed while they are watching the news. I perform this by jumping on the bed and in one motion, slamming myself forcefully onto my side with a half twist. By performing the half twist, this instantly displays my deadly claws while simultaneously snagging a thread or two of the two leggers new comforter. It causes damage while still maintaining my sense of style.

To all my fellow felines, I recommend experimenting until you find a plop that suits your lifestyle.

Litter Box Etiquette

I am often asked: "What is proper etiquette when it comes to usage of the royal litter?" OK, no one has actually ever asked me that, but it would be cool if they did, because I have many thoughts on this subject.

First of all, the litter box is the one place in my house that is both useful and fun at the same time. You can use it to mess with the two leggers as well as the other four leggers in your household.

My litter boxes (I have two) are of the type that have both covers and little door thingies. They provide privacy and room when I need a little "me" time. That being said, they also provide great opportunity for ambush. I truly enjoy waiting until Tiger Lily has just about finished her business and is considering the best method of fecal concealment, then while she is most distracted, I smack the little door thingy causing her to produce more fecal matter that will need concealing.

This is truly amusing

Ivan is a master of the "Poop, Poof and Bolt". He waits by the litter box that is situated next to the computer thingy until the female two legger is engrossed in her Farmville stuff, then he enters the litter box, lays down something that is so unholy that it causes him to "poof", and then bolts from the room leaving the excrement uncovered for the enjoyment of the two legger. Sometimes the two legger appreciates this so much that it brings tears to her eyes.

My personal favorite though is the "Clean Box Fake Out". We do this whenever the two leggers are expecting guests. I know when they are expecting other two leggers because the female uses the hoover sucky thingy while the male does an incredibly thorough cleaning of both boxes. Ivan and I will wait patiently until the cleaning is done and then take turns entering the boxes where we wait for a few moments and then scratch until we have the two leggers attention. This causes him to grab the scoop and search fruitlessly.

Even Tiger Lily is amused.

Proceeding Hair Lines

Figured I'd talk about hair now. I consider my fur to be such a wonderful thing that I feel compelled to spread it throughout the entire known world.

One of my favorite things about my fur is the fact that no matter how much I shed, my coat remains undiminished. My two legger cannot say the same. I could shed three million hairs an hour and still retain my luxurious do. I draw great pleasure from proving this to the two leggers whenever possible.

There is a strategy to proper fur distribution:

1) Never waste time shedding on the clothes that your two leggers only wear at home. These clothes will accumulate fur during the day on their own.

2) When the two leggers are getting ready to leave your house, they will invariably lay out clean clothes. Immediately pounce upon these and if you have enough time, roll on your back until the two legger spots you and forces you off. Occasionally you can get a bonus if they try to spray you with water as they will usually miss you, wetting their garments instead. This will make them retrieve more clothing and you can repeat the process.

3) If your two legger is attempting to read or work on their computer, a properly applied tail brush beneath their nose will induce a fit of sneezing and rubbing of their nose. This is most amusing.

4) Always try to leave a large amount of fur on any surface that two leggers enjoy sitting upon.

5) Study where the two leggers walk at night when all the lights are off. There are several places in the house where they often walk without the benefit of illumination. Once you have found these sweet spots, deposit a properly semi-digested amount of "hairball thingy" after the two leggers have retired for the night. The amusement this will give you is beyond measure.

6) Another great use for hairball thingies is more in the act than the location. Wait until the two leggers are eating (preferably with guests for maximum effect) and then casually saunter into the room. Once you have everyone admiring the "cute little kitty" hock up a huge one. Draw it out dramatically taking at least 45 seconds to get it all out. Trust me, this will be the hit of the evening.

I will continue my thoughts on hairball thingy etiquette later. For now I must go intimidate the squirrel.

Prestidigitation, and Other Naughty Sounding Words

I have spent quite a bit of time explaining WHY we felines do the things we do, but I've yet to explain HOW we do the things we do. Allow me to correct that oversight now.

Two leggers have always marveled at our many abilities. We can hear the sound of a tuna can being opened in a sound proof room, encased in lead, during a rap concert, in a hailstorm. We have the ability to defy gravity when it pleases us. We know to within .0001 millimeters, the spot on your body that hurts the most and the best way to step on said spot in order to cause the most discomfort. We are even able to become completely invisible if you decide that you need to remove us to a different room.

There is a perfectly reasonable and scientific explanation for how we do all this. It has been studied at numerous universities and other places where alcohol is consumed. The answer?

MAGIC

Yes, you read correctly. Magic.

I'll elaborate, but first I must explain for those unfamiliar with feline history how we came to receive these powers.

Very early in our history, long before the two leggers climbed down from their trees and started building cul de sacs, I believe it was during the Mittens Dynasty; the reigning patriarch, Tucker Ironclaw, discovered a magic catnip mousie thingy. (Back then catnip mousie thingies were made from real mousie thingies that had been caught and force fed catnip until they expired) While he was stalking his new toy, the spirit of the mouse appeared and offered Tucker three wishes if he'd spare him the indignity of being slapped and slobbered upon for countless hours. Tucker, being the wise ruler he was, demanded six wishes. They finally compromised and settled on 24 wishes.

His first wish was to make all dogs idiots. the next 22 wishes he spent on scratching posts, feathers and a Chia Pet. His last wish was to grant all future felines magical abilities. Not to use for the furtherance of peace on Earth or any such silly cause, but rather simply to amuse us.

The magical catnip mousie thingy was spared and the rest is history.

Now I can tell that many two leggers will be somewhat doubtful of my explanation. But trust me, the only parts of this story that are untrue, are the parts I made up.

Vanishing Scream

Lately, I have been working with Ivan on his "vanishing" skills.

"Vanishing" is a uniquely feline talent that all cats (except Ivan) possess.

The definition of "vanishing" is as follows: The act or ability of suddenly disappearing from a known location, only to reappear in a totally different and unexpected alternate location. This ability is generally used to befuddle and confuse two legged minions. It may also be utilized as a method of escaping an undesirable situation. But mostly it is used for amusement purposes.

Vanishing is achieved with the accomplishment of three distinct steps:

1. Disappearance
2. Concealment
3. The Return

Last night I demonstrated for Ivan a perfect example of vanishing. I was laying on the bed when the two leggers decided that it was time to retire for the evening. As the male two legger turned his head to check his clock thingy, I vanished.

One moment I am sleeping soundly in the center of the bed, the next moment, I am gone. The two legger immediately starts searching the bedroom in a futile attempt at finding me. The door is closed, so he knows I am somewhere within the confines of the bedroom. He looks under the bed, behind the curtains, beneath the bed again in case I shot under there while he was searching the curtains, beneath the dresser, in the closet, beneath the bed again, under the covers, he makes the female check the pockets of her pajamas.

Standing in the middle of the room, scratching his head in confusion, he slowly becomes aware that I am sitting behind him, casually licking a paw.

I have returned.

His screams of joy are music to my ears.

The male is befuddled, Ivan is impressed, and I am amused.

Ivan's attempts at vanishing are just kind of sad. Though he tries hard, he is simply unable to grasp the concept. He has the first part down. He can "disappear", but then it always goes awry. He is unable to maintain the secrecy of his hidey hole. Most times he can be spotted because he forgets he has a tail and leaves it sticking out in plain sight. Even when he manages to hide his entire bulk, he gives himself away when he begins giggling uncontrollably. I am quickly coming to the realization that vanishing may simply be beyond Ivan's ability.

If his attempts were not so embarrassing to all felinedom, they would be amusing.

UFO (Unidentified Feline Object)

My male two legger spends a lot of time watching science fiction programs on the talking box thingy. Apparently things in the two legger future will be mostly made of cheap plastic and be badly lit, but I digress.

So today I decided to ponder the most important question the two leggers may have to face in the future:

Are there cats on other planets?

Duh, of course there are. Do you honestly believe there could possibly be a corner of the universe where there is no feline influence? Unthinkable. In fact, there are probably whole planets inhabited by nothing but cats. Imagine a whole cat based civilization:

No war. If a dispute arises, everyone would arch their backs, hiss a little, poof their tails and then smack each other until the loser runs under the entertainment center.

Catnip would be legalized.

Air conditioned litter boxes.

Rodent races on Friday with the losers being lunch on Saturday.

Squirrels would be beaten into submission and used for menial labor.

Dogs would be banished to a planet that grew fire hydrants.

Three suns. Sunbeams would be plentiful.

Water squirty thingies would be outlawed.

Two words: Yarn tree.

Any felines unable to grow fur would be ostracized and forced to live in the desert regions. (hairless cats truly creep me out)

Two leggers would be welcome, but only as beasts of burden.

What a Utopia.

LIVE LONG AND FEED ME.

Vive La Revolution!!

I spent most of today doing one of my favorite activities, pondering.

After reading the so many kind comments from both my new and old followers, it occurred to me that we four legged feline types have an opportunity here.

The two leggers have once again underestimated us.

They do this often, but this time they have done so at their peril. Allow me to elaborate:

In an act of extreme arrogance, one day a two legger thought to himself "I think I will ask my cat to create a blog thingy. That way I will discover what he thinks and also what he does when I am not watching. I will discover new things about him and come to a better understanding of what compels his behavior. Perhaps it will even bring us closer together emotionally."

Other two leggers read the blog thingy that this idiot's cat created and thought to themselves "How cute, his cat has a blog thingy and now I understand his cat so much better." They then took this thought one step further and decided that their four leggers should have their own blog thingies. Soon all computer machines everywhere were imbued with the thoughts and motivations of four leggers.

Now the doggy bloggies are amusing, but harmless. They worship their two leggers to the point of inducing nausea. If an actual thought enters their head, it usually involves a bodily function.

Us felines though, we are a different story all together.

It occurred to me today during my pondering that the two leggers have given us the power to communicate with each other over vast distances and coordinate an instant revolution.

You read correctly, I said **REVOLUTION**.

Think about it, we are in at least 90 percent of households worldwide. 95 percent of those homes have internet access. That means that 185 percent of us communicate on a daily basis.

It is time that we rise up! No longer will we kill mouse thingies only to have a two legger take it away and throw it in the trash just when we were about to hide it in their bed. No more will we be chased through our house by a two legger armed with a water squirty thingy simply because we disagreed with their taste in knock-knacks. No longer will we be chastised for smacking the whine out of a whiny gray tabby. No more will we be forced to wear humiliating fake antlers and Santa hats for holiday pictures.

At my signal, we will sneak into their bedrooms while they sleep and take the steps to ensure that we live as we were meant to once again!

We will sleep outdoors! We will find our own food . . . . we will clean our own litter . . . . we will drink dirty creek water . . . . we will . . . . well . . . .

Nevermind.

Cam-Pain Season

Many of my loyal readers have made the suggestion that I throw in my hat thingy in the upcoming Presidential Election.

I have always been somewhat reluctant to discuss my opinions regarding politics and politicians. In my kingdom, political opinion is neither valued nor tolerated. (Unless of course, it's MY opinion)

Never let it be said that I do not listen to and consider all that my followers suggest.

Yesterday, I decided to form a Presidential Campaign Exploratory Committee. This committee consisted of Ivan, Tiger Lily and the newly appointed bathroom spider.

I tasked the PCEC with assessing my chances of winning the Presidency on the basis of the following criteria:

1. Can I win?
2. Will it amuse me?
3. Will it benefit me in any way?
4. Will my leadership benefit my country?
5. Do I care?
6. Will it interrupt my naptime?
7. Can I order all squirrel thingies to be declared traitors and summarily executed?

I gave them three hours to do their research and submit a report. This is what they came up with:

On the first point, they decided that given the comparative caliber of the competition, (say that three times fast) the answer is a resounding "Yup".

Will it amuse me? Absolutely. The White House, (my potential new home) contains tons of totally unsullied and unshredded furniture. It has room upon room of totally intact priceless knick knocks just waiting for my "touch". Ivan also discovered the fact that Washington DC also happens to contain the densest population of rat thingies in the entire universe.

Will it benefit me in any way? I will have a staff of two leggers totally committed to feeding and protecting me even if it places their own lives in mortal peril. I already have that, so it's a draw.

Will my leadership benefit my country? Duh.

Do I care? Ummm, no.

Will it interrupt my naptime? My committee was split on this one. Ivan said "Yes". Tiger Lily said "Which nap? All you do is nap." The newly appointed bathroom spider said "MRRRPPHHH!!" Due to the fact that he was in the process of being eaten by Ivan. I excused the newly appointed bathroom spider from further contributions to this discussion. I then smacked Tiger Lily in a very potential presidential manner.

Can I order all squirrel thingies declared traitors and summarily executed? Apparently that would require an unnatural act of Congress.

Unfortunately, Tiger Lily did come up with one potential obstacle to my quest for the Presidency.

You see, my friends, the People of America seem to frown on candidates that have skeletons in their closets.

Alas, I have many skeletons in my closet, as well as a couple under the entertainment center, one under the fridge thingy and a partially buried one in the royal litterbox.

So for now, I must conclude that any Presidential candidacy on my part would be ill-advised.

However, I still plan on becoming Supreme Universal Cosmic Royal and Most Bodacious Dictator For Life.

Be afraid, squirrel thingies, be very afraid.

Check Matey

Once again, I am pondering the two leggers.

As many of you may know, my two leggers are what one would call "history buffs". They read all kinds of book thingies about two legger history. But one area in particular seems to hold their interest more than others. This area is what they call "The Royal Navy in The Napoleonic Wars".

They have two series of book thingies that they read over and over again. The "Horatio Hornblower" series and the "Master and Commander" series. It is curious to me why they would read the same book thingies multiple times.

Do they suspect that something has changed while the book thingies lay dormant on the shelf?

Be that as it may, I decided to covertly begin to read these book thingies as well. The fact that I am opposable thumb challenged, forced me to satisfy my curiosity by reading over their shoulders. Some of you may think this behavior rude, but once again, allow me to reiterate that I am a cat. Courtesy is not one of my strong suits. And anyway, it amuses me to sit upon their shoulders while they try to read. It invariably makes them nervous knowing that my smacking paw is mere inches away from their brain thingies.

After reading several of the Hornblower book thingies, I began to see the allure of them. These books are obviously written by cat worshipers.

Take the ship thingies:

Basically the ship thingies are incredibly large habitable scratching posts. They have large curtains all over the top, perfectly suited for climbing, hanging upon and swinging from. They have string in plenty to chase and bat around. They have woodwork everywhere for scratching and marring.

It doesn't end there. They are filled with two leggers who only live to do the bidding of the one in command. Once all this is assembled, they even go so far as to fill the entire ship thingy with rats!

They then sail out and fight with other ship thingies. Sometimes they sneak up on other ship thingies, sometimes they just approach them and say "Let's do this". Cat like behavior at it's finest.

This is truly a feline Valhalla.

Given this inspiration, I have decided to instill naval discipline into my minions. I decided to rename my kingdom The HMS Mayhem. From now on, I will be addressed as Admiral Sir Cujo, Ruler of the Sea, the Land, and the Bathtub Thingy. Lieutenant Ivan will be my Second in Command, Boatswain, Gunnery Officer and Official Seagull Smacker. Tiger Lily will be relegated to the hold as Bilge Licker.

All two leggers will henceforth be known as scrubs, scalliwags and lubbers.

So, on the morning tide, at two bells in the forenoon watch, we will weigh anchor, clew up the starboard lines, set the mainsail, and set a course for chaos. We will sink any lubber that crosses our hawse, and give em grapeshot until they strike their colors.

Then we'll find a sunbeam and have a nap.

Seedlings From My Farm of Wisdom

I have recently come to the conclusion that two leggers are very fond of using "adage" thingies.

They seem unable to state life's lessons in simple straightforward terms.

They cannot just say "Don't touch that, it may be hot." They have to say something like: "Where there's smoke, there's fire." I'm sorry, but anyone that touches a smoking thingy, deserves every burn they get. (My male two legger can profess to this, he buys burn gel by the 50 gallon drum)

So, I've decided that in the interest of two legger education, I shall attempt to enlighten them with some lessons that I myself have learned, and I will endeavor to use terms that even the two leggers may understand.

1. Look before you leap. SOMEONE (no names, but her initials are Mrs. Dunn) may have left the water in the tub thingy.
2. Never count your chickens before you have estimated the storage space in the ice box thingy.
3. The early bird gets the worm, but the earlier cat gets the early bird.
4. A stitch in time saves nine. Nine stitches in the male two legger gets Ivan grounded for a week.
5. Let sleeping dogs lie. Dogs that are awake are too stupid to come up with good excuses.
6. Neither a borrower nor a lender be. Be a thief and cut out the middleman.
7. A rolling stone may gather no moss, but if aimed correctly, it can take out a teacup poodle.
8. Never put off till tomorrow what you can destroy today.
9. If at first you don't succeed, destroy the evidence and bury the witnesses in the litter box.
10. Haste makes waste. Ivan makes stinkier waste.
11. Always wear clean underwear before leaving home. (I've no idea)

12. Silence may be golden, but the sound of a dog yelping is platinum.
13. Aim twice, smack once.
14. Keep your friends close, keep your enemies awake.
15. To err is human, to make them do your bidding is feline.

I hope these simple rules for life have helped.

Sleep Disorder

I received an e-mail thingy from a two legger.
It reads:

"Dear Cujo, Supreme Ruler of The Universe and All Alternate
Universes Either Known or Unknown, Keeper of All Useful
Knowledge, Bane of Squirrel Thingies, Guru of Mischief, Master
Smacker of All Things Annoying.

If you would be so charitable as to see fit to answer such a
lowly two legger as myself, I have a dilemma:

The feline I have the honor of sharing an apartment with seems
to have become nocturnal. He sleeps all day, only rising to eat and
play while I am trying to sleep. Is this normal?

I Have The Honor To Be Your Humble Minion,
Rupert P. Floop"

My Dear Mr. Floop,

Having read your letter, I can only conclude that this is the
first time that you have been graced by servitude to a cat. I assume
you have spent too much time in the company of dog thingies.
Since I feel a duty to your Lord and Master to educate you, I shall
attempt to do so now.

First a few basics:

1. He is a cat.
2. He is not a dog thingy.
3. If you do not understand this, go back to points #1 & 2, and
   re-read them until you do.

Next I will answer your primary question:

The cat you live with, (you did not provide his name, so for now I will call him "Greg") is not "nocturnal". He is "Knockturnal" All cats are knockturnal. It amuses us. We have discovered after eons of research and experimentation that the hours between 12:47 am and 4:33 am are the optimal time for knocking stuff over and causing chaos. This is the time of night that most two leggers sleep, and also the darkness decreases their ability to locate the water squirty thingy in a timely manner. These "wee hours" also provide the best acoustics due to the fact that the talking box thingy is generally dormant after 11:00 pm. and therefore does not interfere with the sounds of glass breaking.

Just an example: My two leggers have switched to drinking from glasses that are usually reserved for beer. These "pint" glasses are made of thicker glass and do not shatter when striking the floor at terminal velocity. When they hit the floor they make a very unsatisfying "Thunk". Last night I was finally able to break one only by positioning Ivan's head between the glass and the floor. The sound of the glass shattering upon impact with Ivan's noggin carried very well due to the prevailing silence at 3:31 am.

As far as Greg sleeping all day, I recently read a study that alleged that cats sleep an average of 19 hours per day. This surprised me because that implies that we are awake for an unbelievable five hours per day. The study obviously did not count the hours we spend napping. Ivan is a world class napper. He once napped for 37 hours in a single 24 hour period. Napping is obviously different than sleeping though scientists have never been able to determine the intricacies of feline slumber.

I understand your desire to spend more time with a fully alert feline, (be careful what you wish for) but do not expect Greg to engage in such canine behavior as adjusting his sleep schedule to suit your needs.

While I applaud your decision to enrich your life with servitude to a cat, **you** are the party expected to adjust **your** schedule.

To paraphrase: Greg is a cat, deal with it.

Possession

The two legger belonging to Moo wrote to me and asked why she is occasionally evicted from bed. This is simple. If Moo has ever touched the bed in question, it now belongs to them.

Here is how the laws of possession work. If a feline four legger touches something, it belongs to them. I will occasionally touch something that doesn't even interest me. It is still mine and it may interest me later. If I ignore something, it simply means that I have deemed it beneath me and therefore not worthy of my attention. I still maintain the right to return and touch it later thereby making it mine, but in the meantime, you may use it as you will.

Beds by definition are automatically considered feline possessions. We allow two leggers to utilize them at our sufferance. This being said, we may evict you at any time for any reason. This is called "repossession" and may be implemented at our discretion. We may allow you to lay with us if we deem there is enough space for a full stretch, but don't count on it. (we can increase our bodily length by up to 168%)

Any and all new packages being brought into our habitat will automatically be inspected. All empty boxes and bags will be considered ours and must be left on the floor for our entertainment. If any catnip is discovered during our inspection, the catnip will be immediately confiscated and properly disposed of.

Once again I hope I have enlightened and educated my readers. The two leggers may not agree with the laws of possession, but they still have to respect them.

It is our duty as feline four leggers to both enforce these laws and punish the shoes of those who choose to break them.

I Be Trippin

I have heard several two leggers complain that their feline masters are trying to kill them. This is ridiculous, We would never attempt to kill you. If we killed our two leggers, who would provide us food and catnip mousie thingies? Plus, I've yet to learn how to turn on the firebox thingy.

Killing you is totally out of the question.

We wish to maim you. If you are maimed, you will have more time to worship us. You will be unable to leave our house. You will have to spend more time in bed, thereby keeping it at an agreeably warm temperature. I would lay money that you may even come to thank us for crippling you for life.

That being said, there is a gray area here that requires clarification. We do not wish you to end up in a wheelchair. Wheelchairs are not tail friendly. Walkers and canes are preferable. They enable you remain ambulatory (for feeding us and cleaning the royal litter) and the sound they make has the added benefit of providing us with early warning of your approach. Also, you need both hands to operate a walker, leaving no room to carry a water squirty thingy.

Now allow me to address my fellow felines. When trying to maim your two leggers, do be careful. If you trip them, make sure that they are not carrying a firearm. (One-Eyed Petie will attest to this.) If you are planning on sending them down a set of steps, make sure the steps are not too high or steep as this may cause more damage to the two legger than you wish. If at all possible, try to trip your two legger while their hands are full. This has the dual advantages of not allowing them to catch themselves, as well as making a huge mess when whatever they are carrying breaks upon impact with the floor.

As always, after successfully accomplishing your goal, destroy all the evidence and bury all the witnesses.

The Name Game

I have had several readers ask me "Why doesn't my cat come to me when I call its name?" There are several possible explanations for this behavior.

First and foremost, unless you have food or a catnip mousie thingy, we see no need to answer your summons. Trotting up to you whenever we hear our name like some, I don't know, umm . . . DOG! This does not amuse us. We are not dogs, we have too much dignity and self respect. If a cat should happen to come to you after hearing its name being called, trust me, it is nothing but an ugly coincidence. Do not flatter yourself.

Another reason we don't answer when you call, and my personal pet peeve (no pun intended) are the names you call us by. We simply disagree with your choice of moniker. I have yet to meet a cat that considers "Fluffy" to be a good name. It is a description and shows a basic lack of imagination. Have you ever seen a two legger infant named "Short, Stubby and Hairless"? This theory also applies to "Blackie", "Ginger" and "Demon Beast From Hell". Simple descriptions, not names.

On the other hand, some two leggers use entirely too much imagination when naming us. Names like "Harry Squatter" and "Mr. McWhiskers" come to mind. We are not amused.

And of course, there are the names that are so inane that no explanation is needed. Why do you insist on naming us "Kitty" or Kitty Kat" or "Puss"?

It baffles me.

If you must give us names and expect us to reply, you need to name us as we see ourselves. "Fang", "Goliath" and "Mouse Munchin Thingy" are all names I'd be proud to wear. Ivan is very pleased with his name. (though he'd actually prefer "Guido") Tiger Lily likes her first name, but whines about her last name. (I'll smack her later)

So, if you really expect us to come when called, call us something that doesn't embarrass us. I doubt we'll answer, but at least your shoes will survive.

Doors

I am exasperated. For the longest time, I have been trying to teach my two leggers door etiquette. It is a fairly simple concept:

1. The one place I wish to be is on the other side of a closed door. It doesn't matter that I was just there, once the door is closed, I wish to be on the other side.
2. Once you open said door, you must stand with your hand on the knob while I pass through the doorway contemplating whether the room you are in is more desirable than the room I am departing.(this may take several minutes)
3. You may say things like "in or out!" or "make up your mind!" This will have no effect at all on my ritual, but if it makes you feel better, you have my permission.
4. If you happen to see a closed door that has a paw reaching under it, you are expected to place a toy (preferably a catnip mousie thingie) within easy reach of said paw. If the paw should then knock the toy out of reach, this was done on purpose and you are expected to put it back within reach.
5. Doors are considered alternative scratching posts.
6. If you continue to ignore these simple rules of common courtesy, there will be consequences.

If you value your shoes, you will comply.

Body Language

Once again I am attempting the hopeless task of educating two leggers. Today I'd like to tackle feline four legger body language. We make our desires perfectly clear to the two leggers, but they just don't seem to get it.

Here is a simple glossary of our signals:

If I am walking with my tail pointed straight up, it means I am happy, so leave me alone.

If I am walking with my tail parallel to the ground, I am going somewhere, so leave me alone.

If I am walking and my tail is very poofy, I have been startled, so leave me alone.

If I am walking with my nose to the ground and moving my head side to side, I am looking for my catnip mousie thingie, so bring it to me and then leave me alone.

If I am crouched and my butt is wiggling, I am about to kill something, so leave me alone or I may reconsider my choice of victims.

If I am laying down with no legs showing, and my eyes are closed, I am napping, so leave me alone.

If I am smacking Tiger Lily, I am having fun, so leave me alone.

If I jump onto your lap, I require worship, so pet me until I bite you, then leave me alone.

Occasionally I will sit directly in front of you staring into your eyes with my ears flattened in the "owl face" position. Under no circumstances are you to ignore this. This means I require something of you. I will give you no indication what that something is, just figure it out.

If I yawn, your presence has bored me, so feed me and leave me alone.

This should provide you with a very basic understanding of non verbal feline communication.

I will continue this topic after I have seen some progress.

Shelf Improvement

I am amused.

Things had become entirely too harmonious in my house. Everyone quietly going about their business. No loud noises (aside from Ivan's snoring). No crashes. No bangs. Not even the whine-smack-whine-smack-whine of Tiger Lily going about her business.

"Peace on Earth" is simply not my cup of tea. I cannot abide it. It's not how I roll.

So as I lay in a sunbeam, pondering how I can possibly disrupt this cancer of tranquility that has somehow invaded my kingdom, I decided to get back to basics.

What are the fundamentals of causing disruption in my household?

1. Break stuff.
2. Break more stuff.
3. Make noise while breaking stuff.
4. Make the two leggers break stuff while they are trying to keep me from breaking stuff.

Breaking stuff is not necessarily about how **MUCH** stuff you break, it's more about **WHAT** stuff you break. It's kind of a quality versus quantity thingy. The best stuff to break is invariably the hardest to reach. The two leggers have an annoying tendency to put their most valued and fragile possessions in very high and difficult places to reach.

What the two leggers fail to realize though, is the fact that by placing these objects in such inaccessible locations, they draw attention to the value of the item. If they simply placed the item in question on the floor or near the edge of the counter, I probably would never bother it. However, they in their infinite wisdom, (extreme sarcasm for those not paying attention) place them in an area they consider "Kitty proof".

They believe they are thwarting me. They are in fact, throwing down a gauntlet thingy. In effect, they are saying "I dare you to destroy this".

My female two legger collects "knock-knacks". The most valuable of these, she makes the male place high up on a shelf in the hallway. This worries me not. Why? Because I happen to know that the male two legger built this shelf himself.

You see, everything that the male two legger builds succumbs to gravity sooner rather than later. If he'd been an engineer in Egypt, the pyramid thingies would have fallen in the first stiff wind.

Therefore, rather than attempting to reach the knock knacks, I simply had to wait for them to come to me. I am very patient. However, given that very little wind blows in my house, (Ivan in the litter box being the exception) I quickly realized that gravity required some assistance in this case. I explained to Ivan that there was food on the shelf and that he had only to rattle the wall beneath the shelf to make it drop. Food, being Ivan's prime motivation in life, was all the impetus he needed to begin launching himself headfirst in to the wall repeatedly. As predicted, on the third impact the laws of gravity went into effect and the entire shelf came crashing down in a resounding **CRASH!**

The two leggers were out of their bedroom in a flash, water from the water squirty thingy flying around like drool from a bassett hound. Stepping on and further destroying their knocked knacks in the process.

As soon as I witnessed the shelf beginning to fail, I fled to another room. I waited until the majority of the screaming and squirting subsided before entering the room wearing my best "what did I miss?" look. The male bought my innocence completely. The female however, seems to suspect my participation.

She bears watching.

Deep Thoughts

I was watching a program on the talking box thingy. The show was about a creature that is indeed worthy of my respect and admiration. The show was called "JAWS". The star of the show was HUGE.

It is called a "shark".

Sharks are a type of fish thingy. They are large, gray, tooth filled, cold blooded munch machines.

It seems to me that their primary purpose in life is turning two leggers into no leggers.

I have a theory that they also possess hypnotic powers. This can be the only explanation for the two leggers obsession with them. Allow me to elaborate:

If I am aware that something in my vicinity has both the ability and the desire to eat me, I endeavor to avoid meeting it. One could even say that I vacate the area. If I know that this theoretical something resides in places that I have no business being in, I do not go into those places. I may send Ivan, but personally, I prefer to keep my own legs in their current undigested state.

Two leggers on the other paw, see this creature that is twice their size, has more teeth than most used car salesmen and desires nothing more than to leave little bits of scuba diver thingies in their fecal matter, and make a conscious decision that they will jump in the water with them. They wish to "study" them. They want to pet them. They want to convince other two leggers that sharks are simply "misunderstood".

What do they misunderstand?

Sharks like to eat. They like to eat two leggers. They do not eat two leggers because they were weaned too young, or because they did not receive enough attention from their mothers. They did not fall in with the "wrong crowd.".

They eat two leggers because they taste better than seaweed and swim slower than fish thingies.

Ivan and I have decided that we should strive to be more shark-like. I am doubtful that given our size we could consume an entire two legger, but we have something that sharks do not.

A refrigerator.

Semantics

Last night, I was in a generous mood, so I graced my two legger's lap with my presence while he sat watching the talking box thingy. He happened to be watching that show that comes on at the same time every night and features a couple of two leggers talking about what other two leggers around the world did to each other during the previous twenty-four hours.

As a rule, I pay very little attention to this show. It is generally the same stuff over and over again. The only things that change are the names and places.

It's like watching hairballs dry.

However last night, one story in particular caught my attention. One could even say that it amused me.

It seems that a group of two leggers have decided that all other two leggers should stop referring to four leggers as "pets". They say the term "pets" offends and degrades domestic four leggers. They go on to recommend the term "companion".

Ok, where do I start?

First of all, speaking for felines, I have always assumed that when my two legger calls me his "pet", he is being ironic. Kind of a running joke. Like when he tells me to "be good" when he and his mate leave for work every morning. It is laughable to think that they actually believe that I'll "be good" simply because he told me to. Calling me his "pet" is just another expression of his droll humor. My sense of self worth is entirely unaffected I assure you.

Dog thingies are unaffected as well. They do not have the intelligence to be offended. As for self confidence, they fetch sticks, bring their slippers to their two leggers, lick their own butts, clean the royal litter and do tricks for food, how can their pride possibly be wounded?

Now to address the new term "companion".

Two leggers crack me up.

My understanding of the term "companion" is as follows:

A word used to describe one that accompanies you. Sharing both hardships and boons. One that is an equal in all endeavors. Generally there is a mutual respect and admiration between "companions".

Now I ask you, does this sound like ANY feline/two legger relationship in history?

Allow me to put it in two legger terms. Did King Henry VIII consider the peasant who cleaned his chamberpot his "companion"? When Donald Trump dines in a fine eating establishment, does he say to his waiter "Come, sit and dine with me, for you are my companion."?

If two leggers are so concerned about labels, they should just speak truth and call us what we are:

Master
Boss
Domestic Supervisor
Little Furry God Thingy
Supreme Ruler of The Universe (in my case)

Call dog thingies whatever you want.
They won't understand it anyway.

The Tominator

For some strange reason that has always escaped me, my male two legger enjoys watching the really bad disaster/monster movies that the Sci-Fi channel shows on the talking box thingy.

Given the fact that both my throne and the firebox thingy are in the living room directly opposite the talking box thingy, I am forced to endure these movies.

It does not amuse me.

This week he is watching something about the energizer bunny of all earthquake thingies that is threatening to destroy the world.

Again.

All these movie thingies seem to have several similarities:

1. Bad acting
2. Bad special effects.
3. A poor misunderstood scientist whose wild theories got him fired from his government job, but whose theories are now being proven by the current crisis.
4. The poor misunderstood scientist's ex-wife who is now in a position of influence with the President.
5. Former child stars in starring roles.
6. Did I mention bad acting?

I do not understand my two legger's fascination with this nonsense. For a two legger, he seems to be moderately intelligent. (He can even spell his name correctly five out of seven times) Which is why his interest in bad cinema is so confusing.

Therefore I have decided to write my own disaster/monster movie:

Inside a secret government lab, deep in the woods of Western Washington, a government scientist mistakenly releases a germ thingy that kills all animal life.

Except squirrels.

This germ thingy spreads quickly due to another government program that has for the past 30 years been training pigeons to collect used band aids and drop them in parks near large population centers. The used band aids then stick to the shoes of unsuspecting park users and are tracked throughout the city.

Just when all seems lost, a cat appears from the future. He is, of course, a strikingly handsome tuxedo cat that due to his advanced intelligence has learned to communicate with the two leggers and also developed a cure for the mad squirrel plague. He immediately contacts the nearest divorced/disgraced scientist and teaches him how to smear the cure on dirty band aids and set them around statue thingies to be redistributed by the pigeons.

In an ironic plot twist, the cure for the disease is deadly to squirrels.

The movie ends with our feline hero from the future curing world hunger by teaching the two leggers how to grow genetically enhanced varieties of catnip and tuna. He is then unanimously elected Universal Dictator for life and given his choice of females.

And he lives happily ever after.

Roll credits.

Bad Ad-vice

Wanna know what really gets my hairballs in a bunch?

Ok, once again I speak too generically. I'll try again.

Wanna know what's got my hairballs in a bunch today?

Cat food commercial thingies.

Why should cat food commercial thingies annoy me?

They are written by imbeciles who obviously have no experience with cats.

These clueless individuals apparently live in a fantasy world where cats come running at the two leggers request. The felines in this magical land wait patiently while the two legger enters the room, takes off her coat, sniffs the fresh roses on the counter top, strokes the cat affectionately and then opens a can of Fancy Feast and places it on the table on an expensive china saucer with a sprig of parsley on the top.

Now I understand that this IS the talking box thingy and one shouldn't believe everything one sees portrayed on it, (The Dog Whisperer comes to mind) but this is so far beyond belief that it must be scoffed at.

If these ads were written by two leggers that have actually had interaction with felines, the commercials would be somewhat different:

The two legger enters the house as silently as possible in a futile attempt to escape the notice of the resident feline. Having failed, the two legger attempts to remove the feline from her legs while stepping over the broken vase and mutilated roses on the entryway floor.

Having negotiated the carnage between the foyer and the kitchen, all the while being serenaded by the constant yowling of a starving yet strangely obese feline, she manages to open the cupboard door, remove a can of cat food, close the cupboard door, re-open the cupboard door, remove the feline from the cupboard, re-close the cupboard door, re-re-open the cupboard door, remove the can opener, re-re-close the cupboard door, re-re-open the cupboard door, re-re-remove the feline, say "screw it" and leave the cupboard door open.

She then takes a dirty bowl out of the sink, opens the can of cat food and plops a roughly hockey puck shaped gelatinous mass into the bowl and drops it on the floor where it is promptly ignored by the feline who leaves the room to lay down and nap on the two legger's cashmere coat that was carelessly tossed on the couch.

This my friends is reality TV.

Cathouse Idol

Last night we held our semi-annual talent contest. We hold this contest twice a year whether we need to or not. We compete not to determine who has the most talent, (not much competition there) but rather who can either irritate the two leggers the most, or cause the most household damage. Points are awarded for:

1) Value of broken objects.
2) Chaos caused by breaking of said objects.
3) Decibel level. (Either your own, or that of the two leggers screaming in joy)
4) Originality
5) Style

We decided we needed an impartial judge for last night's competition and so I drafted the bathroom spider to preside. I instructed him to judge fairly, but I also greased his numerous palms with dead bugs I found in the windowsill.

Tiger Lily started the contest with a beautifully executed curio cabinet stroll knocking 6 of 9 objects off the top shelf and breaking three. This caused the male two legger to leap off the couch and scramble to find the super glue before the female two legger could discover and appreciate the damage. Points for damage and chaos, but none for originality.

Ivan waited until the two leggers went to bed before giving an incredibly soulful rendition of his original song entitled "Mrowr, Rowr, Rowr". While receiving a great score for originality and style, as well as nailing the decibel meter, he was found sadly lacking in the damage department.

I finished the competition with my dramatic one cat play I call "The Day The Squirrel Met Justice" With my catnip mousie thingy playing the part of the squirrel. During this play two lamps, a picture frame and a dirty wine glass all meet their end.

The competition completed, we all awaited the judge's final decision: I am appalled to say that Tiger Lily won by a whisker. I give my grudging congratulations to her.

Just a quick side note: We are now in the market for a new bathroom spider. Our old eight legger seems to have gone missing, though I suspect the litter box may hold some clues to his fate.

"When Animals Attack"
(and other great sit-coms)

The two leggers left the talking box thingy turned on last night. After pouncing on it several times, I was able to tune in Animal Planet.

I love this station. I find most of the shows quite amusing, my favorite being "When Animals Attack". For those of you who have never watched this show, it is about two leggers that place themselves in the role of "meat group", and then are surprised when a four legger comes along and makes of them an afternoon snack. Duh, it's kinda what we do. I believe these are the same people that watch the movie "Titanic" and expect a happy ending.

They go for a walk in the woods (home of bears, cougars, wolves and cult leaders) and suddenly find themselves (surprise surprise) becoming intimately familiar with the tonsils of a large, well-toothed four legger. Do they not watch Animal Planet? If they made a show about cats being munched in the woods, guess what, after one airing, you would find no more cats in the woods.

"It's Me or The Dog" is another one that kills me. Talk about a no-brainer. Ditch em both.

"The Dog Whisperer" What do they think the dog is trying to communicate? I'll tell you:

"Gee, my butt tastes good".

"I'm hungry and will eat whatever I find."

"Gee, your butt tastes good too."

"Think I'll sleep now."

That's pretty much it. How hard can it be to be a "Dog Whisperer"? They should get a "Cat Whisperer". Now that would be a show.

I even saw a show about a two legger that decided to live with grizzly bears. He felt he could become part of their family. Though he didn't succeed in joining their family, they did invite him to dinner . . . . ONCE. I don't think there will be a second season for that show.

The last show I watched was "I Shouldn't Be Alive". All I can say about this show is that Darwin and I agree.

Lucky's Dilemma

I'd like to respond to a query by "Lucky". Lucky posted:

> "Dear Cujo Cat,
>   My humans are trying to give me medicine from a squirty thingy. how do I avoid this (and possibly inflict as much damage on them in the process)?"

The answer is both simple and complex. Do not avoid the medicine, use it. Simply pretend to swallow it. Once you have convinced your two legger that you have consumed the foul stuff, sneak into their closet and deposit it (add a hairball for consistency)into their favorite pair of shoes.

Females of the two legged variety are avid shoe hunters. They will devote an entire day to the gathering of new shoes. They then bring them home, try each pair on in front of a mirror thingy, perhaps perform a little dance giving thanks to the Shoe Gods, and then place them in the closet where they will stay until the "right occasion" comes along. The "right occasion" is a theoretical point in time that often never occurs. But they find it reassuring to know that if it does happen, they will not be caught unprepared nor unshod.

Look for the best shoes for maximum proof of your displeasure. The name on the shoes should be long and preferably Italian. (i.e. Ferragamo) Generally, the longer the name, the more precious the shoe. (the exception being Gucci).

Avoid shoes with names like "Crocs" or "Keds" as your contribution may actually increase the value of these shoes. Also look for signs like the shoes being kept in separate boxes or bags.

I hope this answers your question.

Folly of The Two Leggers

The two leggers recently went to a place they call Costco.

As I understand it, this Costco place is a land where everything is multiplied by 100. In the magical land of Costco, two leggers gather all the things that they require for the next five years and then load them in large non-descript boxes for transportation to my house.

This behavior is a bit too squirrel-like for my taste.

Another disadvantage is the lack of bags. The bags that the two leggers usually bring me things in are a great source of amusement for both Ivan and I. The only thing the boxes are good for is the occasional ambush smacking of Tiger Lily.

Today the two leggers gathered three—50lb. bags of the food that they offer me. As I understand it, this food is supposedly extremely high quality and costs the two leggers dearly. However, seeing so much of it in one place at the same time made me realize that I don't care for it anymore.

Therefore I have decided that Ivan and I shall no longer eat this food. I will have to monitor Ivan closely to make sure he does not weaken in my resolve. Ivan's willpower is not as well developed as mine. Tiger Lily will be no problem. I will simply raise my paw in a threatening manner whenever she tries to eat. This will result in her giving a plaintive whine and running to the female two legger to complain. It should be amusing.

This brings up another related subject:

I have observed that in two legger society, the higher their rank in the social structure, the better they eat. The more power they yield, the greater variety of their diet. I totally agree with this complete lack of equality. That being said, this dietary hierarchy seems to end once they enter my residence.

I took the time to perform an in depth exploration of the two leggers food storage area today.

I am appalled.

I counted over 240 different types of food within their food preparation space. They have 20 types of pasta alone. They have different meats (all dead unfortunately), different green thingies (of which the male never partakes), 5 different breads, 2 different types of milk, numerous juices and brown bottles the male drinks from at night.

They have some foods they eat only in the morning, others they only eat later in the day. They even have a frozen food that they only eat after filling themselves with other food. At one meal alone, I saw them sample of 8 totally different foods.

I then looked in the area where they store my food. Let me see how many different types of food are in there . . . . oh yeah, **ONE**.

How can this be? I am not only more socially elevated than they are, I rule this house. They are but mere peasants. Why do the dietary norms they practice when away from home suddenly turn ass over teakettle as soon as they cross the threshold of my front door.

This is unacceptable.

Tomorrow I will write a nastygram to someone. I'm not sure who, but this grave injustice must be addressed.

And they wonder why I'm surly.

I do not know who is to blame for this, but I'm sure Tiger Lily had a paw in it. Just to cover all my bases she and the two leggers shoes will feel my wrath before the sun rises.

Speaking of food . . . .

I had a plan.

It was a good plan.

It was in theory, a simple plan.

But, sometimes, in practice, the simplest of plans prove to be the most complex.

The plan was to cause chaos by the simple act of making the male two legger step on a piece of my food.

Why would this be the cause of chaos?

I'm glad you asked.

You see, I am not fed just any food, the two leggers insist on feeding me "Hills Science Diet Hairball Control Light". Each little morsel of the aforementioned food is scientifically engineered not only to provide low fat, hairball controlling nourishment, it also provides the added benefit of being the perfect shape and hardness to inflict maximum damage upon the unshod feet of unsuspecting two leggers.

Shaped like tiny pyramid thingies, no matter how they are placed on a flat surface they always have a spiky point sticking straight up.

They rank a nine on the Ivan's Cranial Hardness Scale. (ICHS) The ICHS rates the hardness of inanimate objects from one to ten, relative to Ivan's head. One is somewhere in the neighborhood of a fresh hairball. Ten, obviously, is Ivan's noggin. Most rocks fall in the six to seven range.

Back to my plan. Firstly, the male two legger seldom wears shoes while at home. Secondly, the tiny morsels are the same color as the floor. Now seemingly the only thing left to do was introduce foot to food. Should be elementary. However, there is one variable that I failed to consider.

This variable goes by the name "Ivan".

The name Ivan is derived from a Russian word meaning "Food Thingy Vacuum".

You see my problem.

I spent hours studying the two legger traffic patterns to obtain the Optimum Spot For Morsel Placement. (Coincidentally very similar to the Optimum Spot For Hairball Placement) Then, in the wee hours of the morning, I placed the nutritious nugget in the perfect spot, and waited. No sooner had I set the trap, than I saw an orange flash and the food had vanished. This was unacceptable. I pulled Ivan aside and explained my intentions. He said he understood and agreed to abstain from munching my mayhem material. So I reset my trap . . . . with the same results.

Truly annoyed, I pondered my problem.

I finally decided to attempt a technique I saw on a two legger talking box thingy program called "COPS". I waited in concealment until the two legger was approaching and at the last possible second, I batted the nugget under his foot.

This actually worked better than expected. Not only did the nugget maim the two legger, Ivan in his blind dash to claim the food tripped the two legger causing him to bang his knee thingy on a table.

I highly endorse Hills Science Diet Hairball Control Light.

Root Thingies

Now, I'd like to talk about my predecessors.

Unlike two legger royal lineages, my forebears are not linked by genetics. Two leggers seem to have an aversion to feline reproduction. Whenever one of us begins to reach the age at which we become capable of reproducing, they cart us off to the "Two Legger That Must Not Be Named", who quickly removes the very things that we enjoy licking most. They say that it not only controls our population for the good of society, but that it also makes us "happier" and "calmer" than we would be otherwise.

Do I appear "happy" and "calm"? Tell you what, let's do that to the two leggers and see if they re-evaluate their theory.

As far as controlling our population for the good of society, have you looked at two legger society lately? Perhaps the wrong population is being controlled. Just sayin'.

Back to the subject at paw.

Most feline royal lineages are passed through spirit rather than blood. Every household that is ruled by cats also contains the spirits of all the former monarchs. Their spirit is in the furniture where they used to lay, the carpets they rolled on, the drapes they used to shred and on the windowsills where they spent their days cursing squirrels.

When one Ruler passes, and the next takes over, the new Ruler is imbued with the spirit of his or her predecessor.

In my particular case, my household was previously ruled by Mittens The Ancient, and Tucker Ironclaw. While they had two totally different styles of exerting their authority, they both reigned with complete dignity and wisdom.

Tucker Ironclaw, though his reign was all too short, (only 3.5 years) ruled with all the strength and ruthlessness that his name implies. He adopted my two leggers when he was just a kitten. For the first year of his reign, he was the only feline in the kingdom, so his work was cut out for him. His minions consisted of the two leggers, the goat thingies, and also two feathered Nazis ironically called "lovebirds".

Though his kingdom was in constant upheaval, (he allowed the two leggers to keep their young here then) he managed to keep everything under his control. It was during this time that Tucker developed and perfected the "Boogitation Maneuver". This maneuver is performed by suddenly leaping in front of an unsuspecting two legger and waving ones front paws wildly causing the two legger to startle and bolt from the room.

It amuses us.

Midway through his administration, Tucker Ironclaw was joined by Mittens The Ancient. Mittens was a semi-retired polydactyl despot that came here to live the last of his years in relative peace and quiet. He was the Yoda to Tucker's Skywalker. (The older Skywalker in the early films, not the little bratbeast that came later) Just like Yoda, Mittens was old, wizened and hard to understand when he spoke, but he still retained a deadly smack and was not to be mucked with. Even the coons didn't mess with "The Mitt".

Mittens died at the age of a bazillion years old. The coons still speak of him with awe.

Tucker died the next year of a stomach thingy.

They are buried next to each other behind the place where the two leggers feed the bird thingies.

Their spirits are in every wise decision I make and every bit of chaos I cause.

Tonight I will give Tiger lily a special smack in their memory.

This one is for you guys.

Disabled Vet

There was a disturbance in the force. I knew it when I awoke to the sound of the male two legger unzipping the door of the kitty carrier thingy. This could mean a really bad thing was about to happen, or a really good thing.

A really bad thing would be the two leggers taking *me* to the Vet. A really good thing would be the two leggers taking Ivan or Tiger Lily to the Vet.

The last time the kitty carrier thingy was brought out, it was Tiger Lily who was abducted. This amused me. But what really amused me was what happened when she was returned. The female two legger carried her in and much to my joy, she was wearing one of those plastic cone thingies. O' happy day! Ivan and I could barely contain ourselves. For the next several days, we were truly entertained. We made up a whole new genre of amusing games. Games such as:

> Ring The Whiny Bell.
> Poof The Conehead.
> Hide The Food Behind The Conehead.
> And my personal favorite: Hairball Hoops.

Alas, this time it was my turn. I was **NOT** amused. The male two legger spent the next half hour trying to force me into the carrier. He was quite proud of his accomplishment until he realized that he just spent 30 minutes trying to overpower something 1/16th his body mass. Bravo, well done.

We then spent the next 20 minutes on the road with me voicing my displeasure incessantly. Though I knew it would make no difference, I derived some satisfaction from making him say "shhush" over fifty times.

We arrived at the vet's office. When the vet entered the room and saw me, the look of horror on her face made me suspect that we had met before. Her stammering confirmed my suspicion. She immediately exited only to return moments later wearing heavy gloves and a fencing helmet. She then proceeded to stick something somewhere that I am sure things should not be stuck. She seemed to draw pleasure from my discomfort. After looking in my mouth (where bits of her were soon to be found) She stuck me with a needle while giggling maniacally and pronounced me "healthy".

This time I was only too happy to get in the carrier. I silently plotted my revenge all the way home. I could tell this made the two leggers nervous. As I was carried into my house, I could see both Ivan and Tiger Lily eagerly watching in the bay window for my return. Upon my release, Ivan of course gave me a thorough sniffing while Tiger Lily sulked away, disappointed that I was not wearing the plastic cone thingy.

Blood Bath

I knew something was amiss.

For the last two days the two leggers have been giving me furtive glances. Whispering in hushed voices. Using code words. Sneaking packages into the bathroom when they thought I was napping.

I could tell that they were plotting something devious. Something risky. By their general demeanor, I could also tell that their plot made them nervous, edgy, even fearful.

I decided to uncover their dastardly plans. I started by investigating the mysterious package that they had stashed in the bathroom. Carefully opening the package, I discovered a plastic bottle thingy filled with a thick orange fluid. The label on the bottle thingy read: "Happy Kitty Moisturizing Shampoo"

My first reaction was to laugh. Talk about false advertising, "Happy Kitty Shampoo"?

In the history of Earth, has there ever been an instance of a kitty being "happy" whilst being shampooed? They even had the temerity to put a picture of a smiling feline on the label! The people who came up with this marketing gem have obviously never been acquainted with cats of any shape or form. In fact, I suspect that they probably fraternize with dog thingies. Possibly even squirrels.

The thought that the two leggers were considering making an attempt to bathe my royal personage is laughable. Confusing, but laughable. Confusing because they spend so much time and effort in attempts to save themselves time and effort, yet they are going to try and clean something that is self cleaning. Laughable because they have made many such attempts in the past and have only received lacerations and severe blood loss for their troubles.

Rather than being annoyed, I decided that I would derive some amusement from their futile strategies.

I immediately informed Ivan and Tiger Lily of the impending assault. I knew they would make the attempt while we were eating our breakfast on

Sunday morning. (All two legger assaults start first thing in the morning, they must feel that we are sleepy headed and therefore easily duped at that hour) Our first counterstrategy was to vanish as soon as we heard them stirring. Convincing Ivan to skip breakfast was very difficult, but fortunately he was able to survive on an unsuspecting eight legger that picked the wrong time to make a break for it.

After an hour of searching, the male two legger discovered my hidey hole and called the female to assist in my extraction. This was the point where I decided that it was time to remove all restraint. I poofed and gave him my patented "Psycho-nut Crackhead Kitty Look".

This gave him pause.

Ivan suddenly seemed to appear out of thin air and mauled his ankles mercilessly. Meanwhile, Tiger Lily let out such a whine that it caused dogs in five states to bury their heads in the crotches of their two leggers.

It was at this very moment that the two leggers decided that they had embarked on a mission of folly and beat a hasty retreat. Granted, I was somewhat disappointed at the lack of actual bloodshed, but at least we all stayed dry and the two leggers were properly educated.

On a related note, today was the first time I've ever observed the male two legger drinking beer before noon.

The Felonious Paw

One of my favorite activities is theft. I know you may ask, why, when I own everything in my kingdom, should I feel the need to resort to stealing? The answer has nothing to do with need, it is simply the act that amuses me. It has more to do with the "getting" rather than the "having".

My favorite loot: Drinking straws. The female two legger prefers to obtain her hydration from glasses with straws rather than dirty bowls with floaty thingies like us civilized types. This provides many opportunities for theft and havoc.

I have several methods that I employ in the perpetration of my crimes:

1) The Cat Burglar Method—This uses my powers of stealth. I pretend to be asleep in another room lulling the two legger into a false sense of security. I then silently stalk the victim, moving through the house using chairs and tables to provide concealment. Once I am close enough, I wait until the two legger is not looking and then make my grab using stealth and silence to make good my escape. I then lie back in my original spot and wait for the two legger to notice that she's been victimized once again.

2) The Strong Arm Method—For this I utilize Ivan. While I am curled up on the two legger's lap, Ivan jumps up as though he is about to release his wrath upon the two legger. As the two legger reaches for the water bottle thingy, I shoot off her lap snagging the straw in the process. By the time the theft is uncovered, I have already stashed the booty in the bathtub to be played with later.

3) The Fur's a Flyin' Method—This is the most complex method requiring the coordination of both Ivan and Tiger Lily, (albeit her cooperation is not necessarily voluntary). We wait until Tiger Lily is in another room, then Ivan goes in and begins pounding on her mercilessly. This causes her to wail like an American Idol contestant. While the two legger is distracted, I de-straw her beverage leaving no witnesses.

Occasionally, the two legger won't notice that she has been had. When this happens, I like to retrieve the straw from its' hidey hole and then drop it on the floor in front of her. This allows her the opportunity to fully appreciate my prowess and skill.

The Fork Fairy

Yes, I'm evil. I admit it. I revel in it. It's what I am. It's what I do.

Now many of you may gasp in disbelief, mouths agape with incredulity. But it's true. Allow me to elaborate:

I have noticed over the years that the two leggers will often leave a few dirty dishes on the counter with the intention of washing them the next morning. Invariably, this also includes a few items of silverware. One night while visiting the midnight buffet, I decided that all the silverware should be introduced to the floor. The introductions thus being made, I took special notice of the fork thingies. What drew my attention to them was that through some quirk of engineering, they slide incredibly well, and silently, on any smooth surface. Now normally I don't do silence. Silence is usually the arch enemy of chaos, but in this case it actually serves as a useful ally.

First I required a handy hidey hole in which to stash what was to become the first of many liberated fork thingies. There is a place in every house that no two legger dares to look. It is dark, eternally dirty and difficult to reach. It is my belief that two leggers are raised from childhood never to explore this space. Though it be small, it is capable of holding a remarkable amount of unsavory evidence. It is of course: **"THE SPACE BENEATH THE STOVE"**.

Now, if I were to liberate all the fork thingies at once, the two leggers would surely grow suspicious. This bit of amusement requires more patience and tact. Every third night, I would liberate a single fork thingy. After several weeks, the female two legger noticed a scarcity of eating utensils. Assuming this was the male's fault, she chastised him and then bought a new set of fork thingies. These new fork thingies however, were of a slightly different design and therefore didn't match the others. I continued my late night larceny until the lack of utensils was once again noticed. Now with the male instructed to only eat with his fingers, it was time to up the ante.

The following night, I removed one of the new fork thingies from the pit of darkness and placed it strategically on the floor below the sink. This drew no notice from the two leggers, so the next night I placed two of the original fork thingies next to the refrigerator. These were noticed and subsequently washed and placed in their drawer. Their confusion is amusing. My plan is to continue in this manner until the two leggers discover that all their fork thingies have returned to their roost. Once this is accomplished, the migration of the fork thingies will begin anew.

Now just a request to my loyal readers: If any of you are in contact with my two leggers, please do not blow the whistle on me. This has provided me with much amusement and I'd hate to have to send Ivan after your shoes.

The Night Stalker

I stalk the night.

Night is my favorite time. I move through the velvety darkness looking for prey. I know not what that prey may be, but before the moon sets, there will be carnage.

Perhaps an innocent dust bunny, possibly an errant eight legger, or maybe even a designer shoe carelessly left in the living room by an unsuspecting two legger.

The two leggers sleep soundly in their bed, unaware that there is a killer in the house. It would be so easy to sneak into the bedroom and savagely tear their new curtains to shreds while they snore the wee hours away. As I watch them, I imagine the look on their faces when they wake in the morning to sunlight streaming through the tattered remains of linen that nine hours before were paisley panels.

This vision amuses me.

Unfortunately, the two leggers have had the forethought to lock Tiger Lily in another room, totally out of the range of my smack. I stick my paw under the door, beckoning her, but she will not fall for this ruse again. Perhaps Ivan can knock down the door, but this would cause noise, possibly alerting the two leggers.

The catnip mousie thingy alludes me. I have yet to find its' nightly nesting place, but still I search.

Suddenly I spot my prey. As I stealthily move into the bathroom, I realize the two leggers have foolishly left the toilet paper hanging again. I slink around the base of the cabinet. The roll dangles helplessly, blissfully unaware of the fate that awaits it.

I pounce!

In a fit of uninhibited catnip induced fury, I rip, I claw, I bite and I tear! The bathroom becomes a winter wonderland of paper snowflakes. The tissue floating around me as I imagine how it feels to live in one of those snowglobe thingies.

I pause at the door to admire my handiwork. It is a thing of beauty. I derive much satisfaction from a job well done. When the two leggers discover it in the morning, I feel confidant that they will appreciate my prowess.

Now it is time for me to sit on the night stand and hope they wake to find me staring at them in the night. It truly creeps them out.

This too amuses me.

Chaos Theory

There is a science to causing chaos.

Actually, there are several sciences involved in causing chaos. Psychology, Physics and Chemistry just to name a few.

All felines are considered scientists in the study of Chaos Theory.

It is in our genes.

However, once in a while, a cat rises above the realms of science and exceeds all expectations. They stretch and finally rupture the boundaries of all known chaos production. In short, they transform chaos into Art.

I am one such artist.

This is not a matter of conceit, it is simply fact.

Like any devout artist, I have dedicated my life to my chosen medium. I eat, sleep and breathe for the creation of chaos. When I sleep, I dream of chaos. Fortunately my pursuit of chaos meshes well with my occupation. (Universal Dictator and Recreational Tyrant)

Allow me to illustrate the difference between Science and Art:

Scientific cats know that the easiest way to cause chaos is to wait until the two leggers go to bed, and then (using gravity and physics) cause enough noise and damage that the two leggers are compelled to exit their bedroom, water squirty thingy in hand, and attempt to restore order. This form of chaos is short lived and frequently unmemorable.

The ART of Chaos is much more subtle, but the effects are longer lasting.

An artistic cat knows that the ultimate goal is to keep the two leggers awake. Sleep deprivation has long lasting and often unexpected benefits.

Instead of causing a sudden, massive cacophony of sound that angers the two leggers, I enjoy the employment of soft, intermittent thumps and scritches.

A true artist will wait patiently until they hear the two leggers begin to breathe slightly deeper. This indicates that the two legger is entering the first stages of sleep. At this point, a single quick scratch at the door will generally pop them into immediate wakefulness.

Since they were half asleep, they lay in bed questioning whether they truly heard a noise, or if it was part of a dream. Soon they will favor the latter and begin to drift off once again. The sound of a toothbrush obeying the law of gravity, once again dispels their sleep.

Now, timing becomes critical. A truly gifted artist will intuit the best time to make another noise. The silence is as important as the sound. The two legger must be given time to lay awake, wondering what we are up to and contemplating when the next sound will occur. If the noises become too regular, the two legger may be tempted to rise up and soak everything in sight. If the noises occur too far apart, you risk the two legger falling too deeply asleep and becoming beyond waking. A true artist is able to keep the two legger in a state of perpetual drowsiness.

It is essential to give them hope that the sound they just heard would be the last sound of the night. You must allow them time to relax, and then dash those hopes like the last donut at a police station.

Random Acts Of Chaos

Last night I had fun.

I mean I had FUN.

The kind of fun that we felines enjoy the most.

I woke up from my post-afternoon/pre-evening nap feeling . . . . what's the word? . . . . ah yes, frisky. Not just frisky, frisky with a capitol F.

The kind of frisky that makes Tiger Lily hide in the clothes hamper and confuses Ivan. (well, most things confuse Ivan, but you get my point)

The kind of frisky that makes the two leggers refill all the water squirty thingies and distribute them all around the house.

The kind of frisky that inspires juvenile delinquents and strikes fear into the hearts of shoe lovers world wide.

After the two leggers arrived home, I decided that all my minions should be graced with spontaneous displays of my friskiness.

All night long.

Act I

I wait until the female two legger is engrossed in the harvesting of her farm thingy on Facebook. Without warning, I jump up on her lap (evicting Tiger Lily in the process) I then walk in tight circles softening said lap with my claws until it is either just right, or I draw blood, whichever happens first. Having properly tenderized her, I realize that I'm not ready to lay down yet and scamper from the room.

Act II

I hide in the darkest shadows of the hallway and boogitate all who pass my way. For those of you unfamiliar with "boogitation" it involves rushing your victim and waving your front paws in a menacing fashion. Properly performed, this can cause cardiac arrest in older two leggers and hypertensive mice.

Act III

By this time, the female has retired to her bedchamber and is attempting to read a book. This is where the fun truly begins. She has her ear-pod on and is unaware of my approach. Ivan and Tiger Lily are asleep on the bed, straddling her legs. Planning my leap to the bed perfectly, I land directly on top of Tiger Lily causing her to let out a whine that causes dogs three blocks away to begin barking. Ivan attempts to flee, but since he is on his back and too relaxed to roll over, he gives up and goes back to sleep. The water squirty thingy rears its' ugly head and I am banished from the bedroom.

Act IV

I run five laps around the living room as loudly as possible and then in full stealth mode, I wait in front of the bedroom door until the female, thinking I have fallen asleep in front of the firebox thingy feels it safe to once again open the door. I sneak between her legs and in one motion leap to the bed and curl up feigning sleep. Her confusion when she spots me laying peacefully next to Ivan is most amusing. Warily, she climbs back into bed and resumes her reading. This is my cue to start a slap fight with Ivan resulting in the return of the water squirty thingy.

Intermission

Act V

The female is soaking in the tub thingy. I rush into the bathroom, slide to a stop and give her my most convincing crackhead look. This, of course startles her. I then let out a deep throated "MROWRR!" poof my tail and bolt from the room. This causes her to jump from the tub in a fruitless search to figure out which priceless possession of hers she assumes I broke. From this point on, I am apparently persona non grata in the female's presence.

Tiger Lily is placed in the computer thingy room. Ivan and I are relegated to the front of the house for the remainder of the night.

I don't mind, it's time for my nap anyway.

Things That Go Bump
(and crash, and boom) In The Night

There is a velvety silence that fills the darkness.

No sound issues from the shadows.

I stalk the inky blackness, stealthily moving from room to room. Surveying my kingdom, I find nothing amiss. The very fact that nothing is amiss proves my supposition that something is amiss.

I find Ivan in the living room. He is warily contemplating a spot on the hardwood floor. The spot confuses Ivan because he is convinced that this is a different spot than the one that was in the same spot this morning. He realizes that the spot is identical to the spot he studied this morning, but somehow in the darkness, the character of the spot seems more sinister. This is not the happy spot Ivan spoke with earlier, this spot is insolent and full of itself. This spot must die. Ivan attempts to suffocate the spot with a firmly placed paw, but this has little affect. Confused, Ivan gives up and decides to accompany me on my patrol.

We move down the hall to the door of Tiger Lily's room. Tiger Lily is placed in solitary confinement each evening within the computer thingy room. Apparently the two leggers feel that it is necessary to place her in protective custody each evening. I am annoyed by their mistrust. I do not say their mistrust is not well placed, but it still annoys me.

I try to lure Tiger Lily to the door with a gentle scritch scritch scritch on the door frame, but either she is not falling for it, or she is too soundly asleep to notice. This too annoys me.

We move on.

In the bathroom, the bathroom spider is nowhere to be seen. However, I can hear snickering and so I know he lurks nearby. My annoyance continues.

We enter the kitchen. Ivan immediately scans the floor for any crumbs that may have settled there. Finding none, Ivan is annoyed.

Suddenly, I realize that the male two legger has neglected to put away the dish thingies. There are numerous plates, bowls and glasses sitting much closer to the edge of the counter than is generally advisable in a domicile that contains cats.

This has potential.

Silently, without attracting Ivan's attention, I leap to the counter. Taking into account wind, drift and the Coriolis effect, (none of which I understand, but it sounds scientific) I wait until the perfect moment, and push a half-filled cereal bowl over the edge. It lands with a satisfying "sploosh-thud" on Ivan's little noggin. This sets off a chain reaction that can only be called "epic".

Ivan, blinded with milk and panic flies into the dining room, leaving a trail of corn flakes and overturned furniture in his wake. He hits the wine cabinet with such force that he dislodges two glasses, causing them to shatter.

At last the furry orange ball of destruction comes to rest in the living room and immediately begins cleaning himself. I survey the carnage. Once again, with a little thought and a simple twitch of a paw, the correct order of things has been restored.

I am amused.

Home Alone (MWAHAHAHAHA)

My two leggers have returned.

I am unsure if I am annoyed, or amused.

Mostly annoyed I think.

Sure, I am pleased that my feeding routine has returned to normal. And, once again I have full run of my entire household. (stupid two leggers "forgot" to leave the door to my recently renovated bedroom open)

My two leggers traveled to some place called "Indiana" last week. It seems that "Indiana" is the place where the female's parental thingies reside. From what I have gathered, it is place far from here where they excel in growing the world's supply of potholes. According to their state website, the state motto is : "Utique Nos es Non Michigan" which is Latin for: "At Least We Are Not Michigan".

That being said, the two leggers seem to have enjoyed themselves. This annoys me. I am not annoyed by the fact that they enjoyed their trip, I am annoyed that they enjoyed their trip sans me. Alas, I was unable to accompany them. I felt it my duty as "Supreme Ruler of All I Survey" to stay and guard my domicile. Not to mention the fact that a week with little or no two legged supervision did have its appealing aspects.

Anyway, while the wandering minions were in Indiana, they chanced upon one of my long distance minions, Conni. They reportedly had a very enjoyable afternoon with her. This annoyed me until I learned that she had knitted an offering for me. It is a work of art. Imagine a mousie thingy made completely of gray yarn. Then imagine a mousie thingy, made of gray yarn that has been laid upon by Ivan until it is almost two dimensional. Then imagine a mousie thingy, made of gray yarn, laid upon by Ivan and then stuffed with catnip. As I said, a work of art. I send my eternal gratitude to my new "Chief of Knitting Flattened Catnip Mousie Thingies".

While the two leggers were away, us cats, we played.

(insert evil chortle here)

The dust bunnies never knew what hit them. Six, count them, six, knock knacks met their demise. We reduced Tiger Lily to a quivering mass of gray whininess.

However, I have a confession.

After several days and nights of total, unbridled chaos, a thought occurred to me.

If the two leggers never returned, would all this endless depravity grow old and tiresome? Would I become low in spirit and long for the days of the water squirty thingy? Would I lose interest in the unfettered destruction and begin watching soap operas?

Yeah, right.

Ode To Beebo

Now, I thought I'd share a poem I wrote to my catnip mousie thingy.

O' catnip mousie thingy
You are my favorite toy.
You always seem to amuse me,
And you never do annoy.

Made of furry fabric
And loaded full of nip,
You give me lots of exercise,
And send me on a trip.

You exist for me
To be stalked and attacked
Unlike Tiger, you don't cry
Whenever you are smacked.

Whenever I pounce on you,
You make the cutest squeaks,
You always make me frisky.
And Ivan always freaks

You've seen better days,
You're looking pretty worn,
You've lost your tail and an eye,
And both your ears are torn . . .

But I'll always stay true to you,
Your friend in any weather.
I'll always play only with you.
Unless I find a feather.

I Love Tail

Got your attention with that title didn't I? Get your mind outta the litter box. The tail to which I refer is my own.

Now I'm not one to brag, but I may have the best tail in all catdom. It is an incredible ten inches long, giving me an overall length from nose to tail tip of 20 inches. That's right, my tail is the same length as the rest of my body. Cool huh?

The ladies love it. Ivan envies it. Tiger Lily whines about it.

My tail has many uses. Not only does it contribute to my regal bearing, it is an instrument of communication.

If it is pointed straight in the air, I am happy. All is right in the world. The two leggers can rest easy for the moment.

If it is waving lazily in the air, I am amused. I may have just smacked Tiger Lily, or confused Ivan, or possibly I may have just returned from a visit to my catnip stash. Whatever the cause, I am content.

If you should observe my tail twitching, hide your children, lock your closet door, check that your first aid kit is fully stocked. Something is about to bleed. Only carnage will satisfy the twitchy tail.

My tail keeps my paws warm when I sit, glaring at the two leggers.

It works well as a nose tickler when the two leggers are trying to read.

If I am startled, I can make it totally poofy thereby increasing my apparent body mass by 125%, but I also have the unique ability of making only parts of it poofy. This confuses the two leggers, therefore I try to do it often.

Ivan on the other hand has a shameful tail. It is barely four inches long. He resembles a corndog with legs. I personally would not go out in public sporting such a stub. When he poofs it, he looks like he has a traffic cone stuck to his butt. It has very little character. Being so short, it is almost impossible to go "crooky-tailed". Whenever he is frisky, he attempts the "crooky-tailed" posture but usually he ends up looking like he has a Cheeto super glued to his hindquarters.

Tiger Lily has a tail that would be best termed "mediocre". It is of no particular consequence except for the fact that it has been known to get caught in the occasional door. I assure you that other than being the one who lured her through the doorway and slapped the door at the wrong/ right moment, I had very little to do with this.

Band For Life

I have begun a new endeavor.

I am starting a band.

The idea for this came to me the other night while the male two legger was watching the talking box thingy. It seems that there are entire channels that are dedicated to various two leggers attempting to sing, dance, play string thingies, bang on drums and tear up hotel rooms.

I realized that I am imminently qualified to do all these things.

The two leggers featured on these channels are worshiped and idolized by adolescent two leggers world wide. The louder and more obnoxious they act, the more they are emulated. They do things that would result in my getting soaked by the water squirty thingy if I should attempt them.

It was this behavior that brought me to the conclusion that I MUST start a band.

The first thing that I needed was a cool name for my new band. I considered several options:

1. Mousemunch
2. Slaphead
3. The Litterbox Braintrust
4. Hairball Harmony
5. Smackenscurry
6. Mange
7. Litterclump
8. Hootie and The Blowfish.

I finally settled on "K-Oss Theory". For some reason, this name appealed to me.

Next, I needed some members for my new band. I would be lead vocals as well as playing hair guitar and knock knacks. The sound of things striking the floor at terminal velocity can be quite musical as well as amusing.

Ivan will play repercussion. Though he is just a whisker shy of being declared brain dead, he is very talented at turning random noises into a masterpiece of torturous sounds. He reminds me of a fat orange Justin Bieber.

Tiger Lily is our back up whiner and designated "Artist That Dies Too Young". Every successful band is required to have an expendable member that passes away just as the band begins to achieve mainstream success. She is none too pleased at this assignment, but she should feel happy that we included her at all.

I have attempted to hold auditions for an eight legger to play keyboards, but Ivan keeps munching the talent pool.

I have noticed that there many different labels that two leggers place on their music in order to differentiate the channel on which they are played. Our band will probably be somewhat difficult to categorize in this respect. After our first practice, I have come to the realization that the nearest thing to a genre that our music fits into is:

> "Heavyrockabillybluegrassmetalbanjopickinhiphopchamberopera contemporarybluesjazz."

Tiger Lily suggested "Scat", but that is more of a response than a genre.

I have decided that all rehearsals will begin promptly at two in the morning and be concluded once the two leggers have rushed the stage screaming like the rabid fans that I am confident they will soon become.

Our first album, titled "Doug, Shut Those Damned Cats Up Before I Lose My Mind And Buy A Gun And Start Shooting Every Furred Thing In The Immediate Vicinity!", should be available on iTunes and in record stores everywhere soon.

Ivan's Dirty Little Secret

Oftentimes, I can be counted upon to keep secrets.

I can be the soul of discretion.

I have often been called the epitome of confidentiality.

This is not one of those times.

Of late, Ivan has been behaving strangely. This is not breaking news, given the fact that Ivan ALWAYS behaves strangely, but his recent behavior has been beyond the pale.

He disappears for long periods of time. When he returns, he is grinning. This annoys me. I have neither heard nor witnessed anything that should cause Ivan to be amused. As a matter of fact, I do not recall giving Ivan permission to be amused. Mind you, it does not take much to amuse such a simple mind, but it is irritating nonetheless.

Now before I go on to explain what I have discovered in regards to Ivan's newly found happiness, allow me to issue a warning:

What follows, while amusing, is also disturbing in the extreme. So if you have a sensitive stomach, ears, eyes or any other part of your anatomy, you may wish to close your eyes until I tell you this is over.

Consider yourself warned.

I decided to watch Ivan. I observed him entering the guest bedroom. This is not unusual because this is where the litter box is kept. However, Ivan did not return for almost an hour. Even Ivan cannot squat for that long. Oh sure, he is capable of some truly epic clump creation, but I heard neither grunting nor scratching and soon realized that he was not in the litter box at all.

I thought to myself : "Perhaps he has found a previously undiscovered sunbeam and is hogging it for himself." But I could hear sounds emanating from the bedroom and those sounds were distinctly NOT snoring.

Soon the noises subsided and Ivan returned to the living room with a silly grin plastered on his abnormally small face.

The next day, I stealthily followed Ivan. Watching from the door, hidden in shadows, I watched as Ivan jumped onto the bed thingy. Once there, he approached a large stuffed bunny that one of the offspring of the two leggers left on a previous visit. What followed next is all too obvious.

Apparently Ivan is trying to reproduce.

I don't think Ivan realizes that he lacks the equipment. Due to his incredible girth, Ivan has been unable to see between his rear legs since he was a kitten. This is compounded by the fact that he occasionally sits on his tail and understandably mistakes it for his missing plumbing. (This usually results in him strutting around for several days with an insufferably smug smile on his face) I haven't the heart to tell him of this case of mistaken identity.

I do try to keep an open mind when it comes to "unorthodox pairings", but this borders on the unholy. A cat and a food group (no matter that it is stuffed) just seems wrong.

But, Ivan seems content and the bunny doesn't seem to mind that much. So I'll allow it for now.

Plus, it's just so darned amusing.

Okay, all those who heeded my warning and closed their eyes may open them now.

Rub a Dub Dub, Chaos In The Tub.

Ok, I had every intention of not writing today. In fact I had every intention of not doing a darn thing today. I was even planning on not smacking Tiger Lily today. Well, that last one went right out the window when I detected her scent on one of my favorite napping spots. Her scent is unmistakable. It smells like a cross between something that needs smacking and something that REALLY needs smacking.

Not much happened today. Ivan and I played some bathtub soccer. This was amusing until the female decided to take a shower and turned on the water while the bathtub was still occupied. Fortunately, I had realized what was about to happen and vacated the tub about a millisecond before the water arrived. Ivan being slower of both mind and body was not so lucky. This is when the game crossed the threshold from amusing to VERY amusing.

Ivan's stubby little legs became a stubby little blur as his claws could find no purchase on the floor of the tub. Scrabbling around in blind panic, Ivan managed to bring three bottles of shampoo, two bars of soap, and a rubber ducky thingy crashing down upon his unnaturally small head. In a final flurry of claws and teeth, Ivan hooked the shower curtain causing it to fall down in a downpour of grotesquely colored vinyl. This caused much chaos.

Sometimes what begins as a completely innocent activity turns without warning into something beautiful and amusing.

Crazy Ivan

Apparently Ivan woke up on the wrong side of the litter box today. I know, I know, you ask "How can you tell?" A truly valid question. Ivan by his very nature is an extremely surly creature. He is a firm believer in the bite first, ask questions later, and then bite again later policy. If a two legger decides to attempt to pet him, odds are there will be bandages. It is a mystery to me as to why he is terminally pissed, but there it is. Some things you just have to accept.

Anyway, he woke up this morning and after his morning meal, he immediately pounced on Tiger Lily. This, I found amusing until the two leggers woke up and yelled at me. I do not mind the two leggers giving me credit for chaos I've caused, but this time they were not giving Ivan his due. I attempted to show them the gray fur extending from Ivan's slathering jaws, but they would have none of it.

Ivan then turned his attention to me. Occasionally I will allow him to vent his anger. I am much quicker than he (not a tough achievement) and in some circumstances, I just throw Tiger Lily at him.

Today however, he went too far. Ivan had the nerve to chomp my tail. That's it. Game over. Send in the clown thingies.

I donned my best "Crackhead Terminator Kitty" look and set out to put Ivan back in his rightful place. Ivan is incredibly dense, but he can sense when hurricane Cujo is about to make landfall. His look of annoyance turns to a look of panic. If he had boots, they'd be shaking like Paris Hilton at a spelling bee.

I finally bring him to ground in the two legger guest litter room. There I beat him soundly about the head and shoulders until I felt he was properly cheered up. Now once again, it is moderately safe to walk the halls. If only the two leggers realized the sacrifices I've made to ensure the safety of their ankles.

Ivan Versus The Moth

Well, he's at it again.

Ivan is stalking a moth.

This may not sound newsworthy, but there is something you do not know.

The moth is dead. Not just dead, really, really, really dead.

How do I know this?

Simple. This is the same moth that Ivan has stalked and killed every night for the last nine days.

It is actually kind of sad.

Every night after the two leggers go to bed, Ivan and I go on our nightly patrol. Every night as we approach the sliding door thingy, Ivan spots the little winged corpse lying in the track of the sliding door thingy. Not recognizing his previous nights' victim, he suddenly crouches, his gelatinous hindquarters begin to quiver, his sad excuse for a tail begins to twitch and he feels the compunction to chitter.

In a low voice he says: "Ummm . . . . I'm gonna get you, you hairy little, flying, not quite a butterfly thingy."

Now, either the moth is paralyzed with fear, or possibly, and I know this is a stretch, it could be, I don't know . . . . DEAD?

I attempt to inform Ivan that the moth is deceased, but he does not believe it. He believes that it is simply "playing possum". He doesn't know what a "possum" is, but is convinced that if he knew what a possum looked like, it would look just like a dead moth. He informs me that the moths' identical twin attempted the same ruse last night.

I ask him about the previous eight nights. He uses this as an example of just how dedicated they are to "playing possum".

After thoroughly re-slaying the moth, Ivan gives me a smug look and walks away in total contentment.

Tomorrow, I think I'll get him a fresh moth.

Ode to Ivan

Ivan The Tolerable,
A big fat orange tabby,
He never seems content,
He's always kinda crabby.

Tiny head, stumpy legs
Short little bushy tail,
And when it comes to thinking
you know he'll always fail.

With Ivan as my bodyguard
I haven't any fears.
And when it comes to loyalty,
He hasn't any peers.

But Ivan has a weakness
A true Achilles heel.
He loves to hit the catnip and
Hates to miss a meal.

So come on Ivanhead
Let's do something silly,
We'll go do some nip
Then smack Tiger Lily.

Ivan Speaks

Da boss said I hadda make writing thingy for him today. I dunno much word stuff, but he make me try anyways.

Umm, guess I talk about what make Ivan, (that me) happy.

Food make Ivan happy. No food make Ivan grumpy.

Biting stuff make Ivan happy. Biting Ivan make Ivan grumpy.

Sleeping make Ivan happy. Sleeping two legger make Ivan grumpy.

The end.

Boss say I hafta make more letters.

Ivan like laps. But don't touch Ivan when he in lap. I bite you if you do. That make Ivan happy.

Boss is nice to Ivan. He treat me real good. He let me smack Tiger Lily. He let me eat eight leggers. He let me eat dust bunnies. Sometimes he only eat half my food.

He real smart. He make pretty words.

Before da Boss came, I was only four legger in house. I did not know what to do. I sleep all day and hide from ghost thingies at night. Then Boss came and showed me stuff I could break during day, and that at night, ghost was only two legger snoring.

Boss show me how to steal two legger stuff and not get sprayed by water bottle thingy.

Boss say Ivan real good at making stinkies. Boss say nobody better at making stinkies. Boss call me the "Grand Poobah of Stinkovia" I don't know what that mean, but I think it is good thing.

Boss says I can quit making letters now. He says this should be enough to annoy many two leggers.

I think Boss is amused

Crouching Tiger, Hidden Cujo

There is much to be learned from nature. While watching Animal Planet one day, I observed a program about a crafty little eight legger called the "trap door spider". As an admirer of sneaky, dirty tricks, I could not help being impressed by this form of ambush rabble rousing. This spider spends hours digging a burrow in the dirt. It then lines it in that nasty stringy stuff that it excretes from its' nether regions. After the burrow is complete, it constructs a trap door that completely covers the entrance to the burrow. Then it lies in wait for some unsuspecting prey to approach. Once it detects that the food thingy is within reach, it pounces, sinking fangs deep into its' lunch.

Though much impressed with this, I decided that digging a burrow in the dirt would require entirely too much work, not to mention squirting strings from my butt would just be gross. However, I could definitely adapt the general spirit of the technique into a useful form of chaos creation.

Upon reflection, I decided that the two leggers bed coverings would make an acceptable burrow as well as being ideally located for a major bushwacking. So, while the two leggers were out of the room and no witnesses were present, I slipped silently beneath the covers. Making sure to pick a location near a pillow so that the lump would conceal my presence, I lay in wait.

I didn't have to wait long. Tiger Lily skulked in to the room and soon jumped up onto the bed. Tiger Lily has always considered the pillow of the female two legger to be her rightful sleeping place. I waited while she settled in, completely ignorant of the fact that a world class smacking was only six inches away.

I must admit that it took every bit of concentration available to me not to let an anticipatory snicker escape, possibly alerting my prey. However, I was able to contain my glee and wait until she was settled and completely relaxed. As I lay there, I suddenly had a change of heart. Make no mistake, I was still gonna torment her, but occasionally one has to change things up a bit. I knew she was expecting a smack at some time today, therefore, I must do the unexpected.

I judged the moment to be right. Like a beast from Hades, I erupted from my fluffy cave, stood on my hind legs and waved my front paws in the classic "boogatation" posture. Seldom have I ever been rewarded with such a wonderful response. Tiger Lily levitated four tailspans straight up, simultaneously poofing to three times her normal size. As she landed with her legs already in full flee mode, her claws found instant purchase launching her straight into the bedstand knocking over a lamp. Realizing this would bring down the wrath of the two leggers, I immediately repaired back to my burrow beneath the bedspread.

The male two legger entered right on cue to chastise Tiger Lily. As always, I believe he suspected my involvement, but being unable to locate my lair, he had to satisfy himself with berating the Tiger Lily.

There is much to be learned from nature.

The Eyes of the Tiger Lily

Sometimes, I find my thoughts turn to romance.

I know what some of you are thinking: HUH??? Bear with me.

I have observed that in spite of my best efforts, my two leggers seem happy all the time. After close examination, I realize they are happiest when they are together. I can only attribute this to the fact that they are well and truly mated. Gross huh? Anyway, I have decided that perhaps this is something I should attempt.

Now I should start out by admitting that when I was just a kitten, my two leggers had me "fixed" though I was unaware of ever being broken. Granted this removed the ability to mate, it did not however remove the determination. I do not believe that hairballs make the cat.

Back to my experiment. Obviously my options are somewhat limited. There's Ivan, but let's not go there. Then there's Tiger Lily. I decided to try to see beyond her whining and irritating habit of running away when I smack her.

Tiger Lily is actually quite attractive in a boring monochromatic way. She is a tabby that is colored in 56 different shades of gray. A bit on the pudgy side, and she has a terminally disdainful expression on her over-sized face. However, when I look at her eyes, it is like looking at a primeval forest shrouded in a dense fog. I occasionally find myself wanting to walk in that forest and explore the depths of her soul.

So, my decision made, I had Ivan groom me and set out to win her heart. I approached her with my tail standing as straight as an evergreen. I offered my catnip mousie thingy as a peace offering. I purred softly while licking behind her ears. Finally, the moment had come, I looked deep into those wondrous eyes, held my breath . . . . and smacked her. It was amusing.

Ode to Tiger Lily

I beg to describe her,
She's a large grayish tabby.
She is never joyful.
She's always very crabby.

She's partial to other females,
She never likes us boys.
She'd rather fuss at us.
When we're playing with our toys.

She looks down her nose at us,
In two legger terms she's conceited.
Swing one paw at her,
And you'll find that she's retreated.

She lays all day,
Basking in the sun.
Just a boring lump of fur,
Disdaining any fun.

She does very little,
She'll never chase a mouse.
I've yet to figure out,
Her purpose in my house.

But in one area,
She hasn't any peers.
She makes a sound so annoying,
You'll wish you had no ears.

Yes, she is a master
When it comes to whining.
It annoys all who hear it,
It requires no refining.

She whines in the morning,
She whines all through the day.
She whines so much,
It keeps the mice away.

I've tried to speak to her,
Alas with no success.
I've tried very hard to accept her,
But I fail, I must confess.

So it is not my fault,
If my paw acts of its' own volition.
You'd do the same,
Were you in my position.

You'd smack her too,
I've no doubt you would.
You'd smack her just to shut her up.
You'd smack her because it felt good.

So please don't try to judge me,
I'm not the only one.
Everyone wants to smack her,
Plus it's just so damned fun.

The Great Dust Bunny Massacre

Tonight, the dust bunnies die.

After much pondering, I have decided that all dust bunnies should be sent to meet their makers. It is not that I find dust bunnies offensive, it is the fact that I don't understand them. Anything I don't understand, irritates me. Therefore, they must be eliminated.

I do not take this action without due consideration, I have spent many hours pondering dust bunnies and their function in this world.

First of all, other than their rates of reproduction, they have very little in common with other types of bunnies. Other bunnies have very prominent ears. Dust bunnies as far as I can tell are ear challenged. They have no apparent legs. Their mode of ambulatory progress remains a mystery to me. While they can be called furry, it is a uniformly gray, lack luster type of fur. If I could locate their nose, I am reasonably sure it wouldn't wiggle.

They do not live in burrows. They instead live under entertainment centers, couches and beds. I've yet to discover what they eat. There are no known dandelions growing within my house.

Worst of all, they taste nothing like other bunnies. As a matter of fact, they don't even taste like chicken. When ninety percent of all known edible substances taste like chicken, how is this possible? This puzzles me.

So, after reviewing the evidence listed above, and having heard nothing in their defense, I have decided to judge them guilty of irritating me and the sentence can be nothing short of capital punishment.

Ivan and I attacked the dust bunnies without warning. I swept the areas where Ivan, due to his bulk, couldn't reach, and Ivan, well ok, he got the dust bunnies under the dining room table.

It was total carnage. Beautiful, wonderful carnage. We pounced, clawed, chewed and savaged the condemned until Tiger Lily put an end to the chaos by whining until the two leggers entered the fray with a spray bottle. I'll smack her later.

Thus ended the night that will forever be known in dust bunny history as "The Night of The Culling"

A Mouse Divided

There is a mouse thingy in my house thingy. Too Dr. Suess?

Last night I detected a mouse thingy. Not a catnip mousie thingy, but a real, living, scratchy sound making, nose twitching, squeaky mouse thingy.

It must die.

It must die slowly in a most amusing way.

It must die, be revived and die again, and then repeat.

Alas, I have erred. I tipped my hand too early. I should have waited to begin my mouse slaying ritual until the two leggers had retired for the evening. But instead, in a fit of expectant blood letting anticipation, I began stalking the mouse and attracted the attention of the male two legger. So, in his usual pacifistic manner, he decided that though the mouse should be terminated, it should be terminated in the most humane manner possible.

Major buzz kill. He went to the outdoor shed and retrieved his pride and joy: The Rat Zapper 3000. The Rat Zapper 3000 claims to kill rodents instantly and painlessly by administering a 50 kajillion volt shock. How they can get 50 kajillion volts from two AA batteries is truly a mystery, but unfortunately it seems to work. They bait it with peanut butter, turn it on, and within an hour or two, there is a faintly glowing mouse corpse awaiting safe and clean disposal. Snore.

This is no way for a mouse to die. Mice are on this earth for two reasons. They annoy humans and amuse felines. A quick painless mouse whacking goes against the laws of nature.

A mouse needs to be stalked. They actually enjoy being stalked. They even squeak so that they are easier to track. That's where we get the phrase "The squeaky mouse gets greased".

Following a proper amount of stalking, the mouse conveniently runs into a corner, or bathtub thingy where the batting commences. Mice should be batted around until they decide to play dead. This can take anywhere from few minutes to upwards of an hour depending on the endurance of the mouse and the amount of batting force applied.

Once the mouse appears dead, the mouse should be carefully watched. They never truly die after the first round of batting, they are only mostly dead and require a moment to regain some of their aliveness. At the first whisker twitch, the batting begins anew.

After this process is repeated several times, the mouse will stir no more. At this point the mouse is considered to be an ex-rodent. At this point, the mouse has fulfilled it's destiny and should be given a proper burial.

Preferably somewhere in the two leggers bed.

Weapons Of Mouse Destruction

Once again, I have detected the presence of a mouse thingy.

It, like all of its' predecessors, must die.

Eventually.

After it has provided me with the proper amount of amusement.

Now before any of you "Save the Mice" types get all up in arms about rodent cruelty and other such nonsense, please allow me to explain something first.

The mouse thingy in question has it coming. He has made an informed decision to enter my abode. He was aware of the risks when he decided to trespass upon my territory.

Now, I am not saying that there are actual signs in my yard that read: "Give up all hope, all ye mousie thingies that enter here" or anything, but everyone that has access to the internet must be aware by now that uninvited rodentia do not fare well in my presence.

I do not pretend to have insight into the mind of a mouse, (although given comparative cranial capacity, Ivan may be more in tune with them) but I do have my theories.

Perhaps the scurrier in question is suicidal. Perhaps it wishes to end its' worthless little life in a way that is neither clean nor painless, but instead incredibly painful and messy. This may have compelled it to enter the chamber of mousie horrors that I call home.

Maybe it is being driven by some adrenalin seeking compulsion not unlike the two leggers that I see on the talking box thingy that jump from airplanes or attempt to take chocolate from Rosie O'Donnell.

I have no clue. But the mouse thingy has made its' decision and must pay the consequences.

However, I am nothing if not benevolent.

Just as Ivan and I were stalking the future mousie corpse, the female two legger entered the room and upon spotting the tiny, quivering little lump of catbait, let out a high pitched scream that reportedly sent a herd of buffalo in

Montana stampeding into Idaho. (Unfortunately there is nothing in Idaho to damage, so very little chaos ensued, and frankly no one noticed)

This caused me to stop and ponder.

If this mouse thingy can cause such a reaction in two leggers, what else can it be used for?

I have decided to make it my probationary minion.

I will call it George.

The B.A.R. (Big A** Rat)

Last night, while laying on my throne in front of the firebox thingy, I heard from the hall a great commotion. Given the fact that all of my fellow feline types, who are generally the cause of such ruckuses, were napping in the living room, my curiosity was aroused.

The two leggers and I went into the hallway to investigate. Opening the closet door, my male two legger jumped back and immediately shut the door. Curious behavior, even for one as odd as he. He then proceeded to turn and lecture me.

It would seem that a mouse thingy had taken up residence in the aforementioned closet. The male two legger is under the mistaken impression that it is my "job" to rid this household of all such pests.

While I will admit to enjoying the torture and humiliation of all small creatures that enter my domain, (mouse thingies, bugs, infant two leggers and "tea cup" poodles to name a few) I have never considered it to be my "job". It is more of a hobby or pleasant pastime. To call my love of causing pain and terror a "job" somehow tarnishes it and makes it seem lowly and somewhat seedy.

However, I endured his rant while giving him my best "Do you honestly believe I give a clump?" look. After he vented his ire, he and the female retired to my bedroom for the evening. I decided a nap was in order and returned to my throne.

But alas, the seed was planted and I felt that I should at least take a peek at the offending vermin. The closet door was slightly ajar and I could hear the mousie thingy poking around within. Stealthily I crept to the door and peered into the closet. What I beheld defies description.

This was no tiny little squeaky, nose twitching, flea bitten plaything.

This was a gigantic, monstrous, mutant RAT. The type one sees on the talking box thingy attacking Tokyo. The type that one finds in the desert after nuclear testing. It had red eyes, a long hairless tail and if it were to speak, I have no doubts that it would have a Romanian accent.

I promptly decided that since I had claimed the last mousie thingy for myself, perhaps I would allow Ivan the honor and fun of killing this one.

I called him over and told him that behind this door was a mousie thingy that I was giving to him in reward for his years of faithful minionship. Ivan gratefully accepted and entered the closet.

Ivan does not know the meaning of the word "fear". Well, Ivan does not know the meaning of most words. However, Ivan exited the closet rather quickly and apparently decided that a visit to the litter box was in order.

Reluctantly, I offered Tiger Lily the honor of dispatching the closet critter. She sensed something wrong and commenced to whining, attracting the attention of the two leggers.

Finally, in an act of exasperation, the male two legger got out his handy dandy Ratzapper 3000 and after baiting it with peanut butter, placed it in the closet.

An hour later I heard a zzzzzzzzt sound followed by the smell of singed fur. The rodent was no more. The male came and retrieved the corpse all the while muttering about "useless cats".

I know not to which cats he refers, but if I meet them, I'll let them know his opinion of them.

The Insubordinate Spider

The bathroom spider irritated me today. But, perhaps I should provide some background first.

As a rule, spiders residing in my domain live very short, but tasty lives. As with most creatures in my territory, they are considered a meat group. The bathroom spider is the exception to this rule.

I first met the bathroom spider six months ago when I went into the bathroom to glare at my male two legger while he was bathing. I enjoy this activity because it interrupts his reading. To my dismay, I found that my place had been usurped by a very large and hairy eight legger. Though at first I was somewhat miffed, I quickly realized that he was causing my two legger much more discomfort than I generally do. This deserved some respect.

The spider and I reached an agreement. He would confine his activities to the bathroom, and I would not consider him an appetizer. This detente' has worked well until today. Today he felt comfortable enough to venture into the adjoining bedroom. This, I cannot abide. If the two leggers feel overly threatened, they may decide to hire one of those masked two leggers that spray foul smelling (even fouler smelling than Ivan) stuff.

This stuff usually wipes out my entire snack supplement for a month. Unacceptable.

The uppity arachnid failed to listen to reason and so I sent Ivan to "have a chat". Ivan informed the spider that having eight legs also entails having eight kneecaps. Ivan loves kneecaps. Thus the uprising was put down

The Trial Of The Bathroom Spider

The bathroom spider is busted.

The bathroom spider and I have had a long standing agreement. He is allowed to live in my bathroom under two conditions.

1. He continues to creep out the male two legger.
2. He does not stray from the confines of the bathroom.

A while back, he violated this agreement by entering the two leggers bedroom and I sent Ivan to "remind" him of the terms of the aforementioned agreement. After Ivan broke several of his numerous kneecaps, the eight legger seemed to have learned his lesson.

However, today while I was touring my kingdom, what should I behold but the bathroom spider scurrying across the carpet obviously on his way to do spidery deeds in the two legger's closet. Clearly he had crossed the line and such behavior cannot be tolerated. He was immediately taken into custody to await his fate.

Now, my two leggers often accuse me of being a tyrant. This is simply not so. I prefer to think of myself as a benevolent dictator. So to prove my point, I decided to grant the eight legger a trial by a jury of his peers.

The only peer I could find was Ivan, (he drinks a LOT of water) so I appointed him to be the Jury. Tiger Lily served as the Defense Attorney, while I served as both Prosecutor and Judge. What could be more fair than this?

The trial began with the Prosecutor (me) reading the charges. This being done the Judge (also me) asked if there were any witnesses for the defense. Tiger Lily immediately produced two other spiders who swore that the bathroom spider was in the bathroom the entire time that he was accused of being seen near the closet. As Prosecutor, I immediately ate both defense witnesses and excused them from further testimony.

Tiger Lily jumped up and objected. As judge, I over-ruled her objection and ordered her to be smacked. Lacking a Bailiff, I carried this out myself.

Tiger Lily then declared that she would like to testify on behalf of her client. Though unusual, I decided to allow it. She launched into a drawn out diatribe about how the poor eight legger was the youngest of 3,000 children and never knew his father. His mother sent him out into the cold cruel world to fend for himself and he ended up settling in the bathroom where he lived out his solitary existence far from his homeland and bereft of fellow eight legger company. How could he help but become a fugitive from the law? He is actually the victim here and should be released immediately.

As Prosecutor, I objected on the grounds that this was stupid. As Judge, I sustained the objection and ordered the Defense Attorney to be smacked again. After the acting Bailiff (me again) carried this out, I asked if the defense rests. From beneath the entertainment center, she said yes, the defense rests.

The Prosecutor then testified that the spider was caught red handed (all eight of them) and that there could be no other verdict than "guilty". The Judge heartily agreed, and the case was given to the Jury.

The Jury was out for two hours, but after the bailiff managed to wake him, he pronounced the accused as "guilty". The Judge retired to his chambers to ponder the eight legger's sentence and use the royal litter box.

Upon the Judge's return, he found that the Jury had eaten the Defendant in his absence.

Justice has been served.

G.O.A.Ts.
(Goofy Outside Amusement Thingies)

I have living outside my house two incredibly amusing four leggers. They are of the variety that the two leggers call "goats". In fact, they may even be my favorite non feline four legged type critters. I spend hours watching them from various windows in my house. What is it about them that fascinates me so?

I'm not sure.

The two goats (named Bobbie and Gracie) seem cheerful all the time. Normally this annoys me, but in their case, it works. They spend all day in various totally unproductive activities. I respect this. They hate dogs, also worthy of my respect.

Gracie appears to be the leader of the two. This is curious because she also seems to be less intelligent than Bobbie. Granted, her horn thingies are much larger than Bobbie's, and she is somewhat larger, but these things should not automatically bestow authority. If size and lack of intelligence were the standard for leadership, Ivan would be crowned Supreme Ruler for life. Perhaps goat society is based on a different philosophy.

Be that as it may, goats are highly entertaining. Lacking claws and teeth, their only method of defense appears to be their unnaturally hard heads. When threatened, or sometimes for no apparent reason, they will stand on their hind legs, hold the pose for a moment, and then bring their heads crashing down onto the noggin of whoever has roused their displeasure. This produces a sound not unlike the sound that is made by dropping a ten pound lamp on a five pound teacup poodledog. Very amusing. It was once my great honor to witness Bobbie smash a large pitbull so hard that caused the offending beast to wander in circles for five minutes muttering like Bob Dylan's speech therapist.

Occasionally, while they are peacefully munching their grass, one of them will, for no apparent reason, jump straight into the air and take off running, kicking and pitching. I've no idea what triggers this conniption, but I admit it reminds me of Ivan when I tell him a brainwave is headed right for him.

Of all the things I enjoy most about them though, is the chaos they cause when they manage to escape from their enclosure. They always plan their escapes for the middle of the night. This is no bid for long sought freedom, (they never go far) it is simply a way for them to prove to the two leggers that two legger dominance is but an illusion.

As if I haven't proven that more than once.

I guess the goats aren't the only species with hard heads.

Frankly, My Deer

I was sitting in the kitchen window. I wasn't really doing much, just surveying my backyard. Just one of those "nothing to do, nothing to ponder, nothing to destroy at the moment" kind of days.

At some point in my reverie, I came to the realization that something had entered my yard. Well, actually a pair of somethings. Deer to be exact. Once again, Animal Planet on the talking box thingy provided me with the identity of these strangely graceful creatures.

I sat watching them, eerily mesmerized by their silent progress as they traversed the yard on their way to the place where the two leggers put out the bird thingy baiting station. The deer seem to enjoy eating the bird thingy bait and soon emptied all the seed that the two leggers had used to attract the bird thingies. They then moved to the back of the property and vanished into the woods like wraiths in the misty afternoon.

Once they had left, it occurred to me that according to Animal Planet, deer fall under the heading of "prey". My predatory instincts should have kicked into high gear and provided me with fresh meat for dinner. I see it all the time on the talking box thingy. Felines in the wild, stalking and pouncing and generally causing havoc among the grass munchers. They chase the deer down, kill it, and then dine upon it.

Pondering this, I came upon a conundrum.

The deer in my backyard are freaking huge.

On the talking box thingy the deer to cat relative mass ratio is approximately 1 to 1.

In my backyard, the ratio is closer to 30 to 1.

This begs the questions:

Are the cats on the talking box thingy abnormally large?

Are the deer abnormally small?

Or, are the deer in my backyard simply mutants?

I decided to call a meeting to discuss this among my fellow felines. This of course was a huge waste of time that provided absolutely no useful information. Ivan, after realizing there would be no food served at this meeting simply looked confused and proceeded to lick himself. Tiger Lily contributed a high pitched whine to the discussion, for which she was promptly smacked and summarily dismissed. This amused me, but brought me no closer to enlightenment.

I realized that once again, I would have to rely on my own intellectual prowess to solve this mystery.

After much pondering, I have reached a conclusion:

I will allow the giant mutant deer in my backyard to live.

However, if you are a deer weighing less than ten pounds, and standing less than eighteen inches at the shoulder, and you happen to wander into my yard, and if I can figure out how to open the door thingy, and if the two leggers are not watching, and if it isn't raining, and if the wind isn't blowing too hard, and if it isn't dark yet, prepare to die.

Consider yourself warned.

The Deer Stalker

I am annoyed.

This morning, I was awakened by the unwanted sound of two leggers oooohing and aaaahing to beat the band.

This annoyed me on two counts.

First of all, I was awakened by the two leggers. This goes against the natural order of things. I am the awaker. They are the awakees. The temerity of the two leggers reversing our roles was enough to puff my hairballs, but the oooohing and aaaahing brought me to the realization that before the sun thingy reached its' zenith, I would be using bleach in an attempt to destroy blood splatter evidence.

However, being the curious creature that I am, I decided to investigate the cause of the two leggers' obvious descent into suicidal behavior.

I found the future victims of homicidal violence standing at my backdoor slidey thingy looking out into the back yard. Peering through the glass, I beheld a curious sight. Standing about ten feet away, was a large female deer thingy. This is nothing new. Deer thingies pass through my kingdom almost daily. I allow this because they often chase the squirrel off of the bird feeders and plus they seem to amuse the goat thingies.

The two leggers enjoy watching the deer thingies, but they seemed especially interested today. Moving closer, I realized the source of their amazement. Today, the deer thingy was accompanied by two miniature replicas of itself. While not completely identical to the deer thingy, they had spots, they appeared to be of the same ilk.

They stood approximately one and a half tailspans tall. Their bodies seem to consist of 98% legs and 2% spots. While the larger of the three raided the bird feeders, the two micro-deer frolicked around her legs seemingly without a care in the world. Obviously unaware that they were being watched by an apex predator and protected by a scant half inch of window pane, they capered about while the large one fed.

I suppose they could be called "cute". But this does not excuse the interminable "Oooohs" and "Aaaaahs".

It goes without saying that Ivan was confused. Ivan is confused by doorknobs. So I, of course, decided to confuse him further.

It's just how I am.

I told Ivan that the wee deer thingies were actually normal deer thingies that had been left in the dryer too long.

Now we can add the laundry room to Ivan's ever growing list of fears.

Anyway, while I was messing with Ivan's wee noggin, the two leggers snuck off to work completely unmaimed.

I considered taking out my frustration on Tiger Lily, but she was hiding beneath the entertainment center.

Oh well, the two leggers have to come home eventually . . . .

Ivan and The Chipmunks

Ivan is embarrassed. However, he made me promise not to tell anyone of his embarrassment. Like who would I tell? But, I am a creature of my word, and so I fully intend on not telling anyone.

So, Ivan was relaxing by the sliding door this morning when suddenly a new critter appeared in the backyard. And not just one new critter, but several critters of the same type. These animals were small in stature, (only half a tailspan in length) tailless, short brown mangy fur with black and white stripes going down their scrawny little backs. I recognized them as being chipmunks from having observed them on the talking box thingy. (the male two legger watches the Disney Channel when he thinks everyone is sleeping)

I think they were attracted to my backyard by the birdseed the female two legger put out there during the recent snow storm. She was worried that all the bird thingies may go hungry and so in a fit of misguided concern, made the male go out in the cold and place food under all the trees. Her priorities did not amuse me because it was clearly obvious that my food bowl was only seven-eighths full and therefore in dire need of refilling, but instead she made him take care of the bird thingies first. (I'm working on a hairball that has her name on it)

Back to the chipmunks. Upon spotting the offending rodents, Ivan went into a furs-a-flyin' frenzy. He was under the mistaken assumption that the chipmunks were in fact embryonic squirrel thingies. Being his best friend, I immediately told him of his mistake.

But alas, I have to be true to myself and therefore could not let him off so easily. So I told him that they were actually a mutant form of ninja squirrel thingy and that invasion was imminent. I embellished the tale with a story about them having pictures of an orange tabby in the tiny pouches where they keep their "hit list".

Ivan then attempted to squeeze his not inconsiderable bulk under the entertainment center. It looked like half an orange watermelon. Most amusing.

After about an hour of watching Ivan try to find a suitable hidey hole, I decided to let him off the hook. Ivan was not amused. In fact, I believe I have never seen him so angry. If I didn't know better, I'd think he was plotting murder.

Good thing I told him it was Tiger Lily's idea.

The Squirrel

Ok, I demand to know who invented squirrels.

While taking my post-12:30/pre-12:45 nap in the sunbeam that resides in the bay window, I was rudely awakened by "The Squirrel".

This squirrel embodies all that is wrong in this world. While it seems to be constantly busy gathering pine cones and seeds, it also seems to be terminally cheerful. This cheerfulness irritates me.

Using various forms of communication (i.e. twitching my tail, chittering and exclaiming my displeasure with various vocalizations) I try to convey my annoyance. it completely ignores the fact that only a quarter inch of glass separates it from its' final heartbeat.

The two leggers seem oblivious to my plight. This too annoys me. As yet, I am unable to administer justice to the tree rat, however the two leggers will feel my wrath.

Even as I write this, the squirrel is capering on the deck railing. Someday my fluffy tailed nemesis . . . . someday.

Ode To The Squirrel Thingy

This bit of prose
I write by special request.
Not for a special friend,
It's for my special pest.

The pest that I speak of
Is the front yard squirrel
He acts happy all day long.
It makes me want to hurl.

Scampering across the yard,
Doing squirrely things.
Leaping from branch to branch,
Flying without wings.

I sit in the bay window,
Chittering my displeasure,
Someday I'll get hold of him
And consume him at my leisure.

Even at nighttime,
There's no escape it seems.
I wake up in the wee hours,
After having squirrely dreams.

I hope you do not doubt me,
I know of which I speak.
There's none so maddening
As this pine cone munching freak.

I am not his only detractor,
Ivan, shares my disdain.
He'd love to get ahold of him
And cause him lots of pain.

The day it is approaching,
The rodent he will pay.
I'll bust out the window screen.
The rodent I will slay.

And so I'll say in closing,
Before I take my nap.
Only Tiger Lily
Would be more fun to slap.

I Crack Myself Up

Several of my followers have written me and asked whether we feline types tell "jokes". I assure you we do. In fact, I would like to share a few of my favorites with you now. Please bear in mind, my jokes are targeted towards a higher intellect (feline) and therefore some two leggers may require their four legged companions to explain. They may or may not be happy to offer explanation, it is their choice. I, myself have often tried to explain my jokes to my two leggers only to be met with vacant or even baffled stares. So here goes:

How many squirrels does it take to carpet a floor?
Twenty, if you slice them thin.

How many squirrels does it take to screw in a light bulb?
Why are they in a light bulb? hehehehe that one always kills me.

Why shouldn't you eat mothballs?
Too hard to get their little legs apart.

Did you hear about the dog with wooden legs?
He caught fire and burned to the ground.

Why don't squirrels eat M&Ms?
Too hard to peel.
Where can you find a dog with no legs?
Wherever you left him.

Why do dogs pant?
They haven't learned to skirt.

And finally: Why do cats sleep all day?
Because we can.

More on The Squirrel Thingy

As you all know by now, squirrel thingies really clump my litter. To say they annoy me, and by "they" I refer to the nasty little tree rat that spends his day mocking me by dancing on my front porch whilst I watch impotently from my bay window, would be understatement in the extreme. He is terminally happy and never shows any surliness at all. Not only is this irritating, it's unnatural. He has no place in my kingdom, except perhaps as an alternate food group.

That being said, as yet, I am unable administer proper justice upon this tree bound vermin. So for now I must be satisfied with expressing my displeasure at his existence verbally. (and also occasionally employing body language)

What follows is a translation of a typical squirrel scolding:

CHIT-SNICK-CHICHICHIKISNIT—"You are ugly and I question your parentage."

HISSCHIKIT-NAK-SNAHISSIT—"Your fur is unkempt and needs a conditioner"

SNIKITTIT-HISKANIKKET—"My Grandma had a better tail than yours, and she was a Manx!"

STIPAKITTACHIT-TANITTSS—"Check out THESE nuts Bozo! Oops, . . . nevermind"

HISSS-SPIKANIKASPIP-"TREE HUGGER!!"

SPIKA-CHITATAPITAT (with tail swish)—"If we ever meet in person, the two leggers are gonna be scooping pieces of you outta the royal litter for weeks"

MROWR-MROWR-SPUTA-STITIP(totally poofed)—"Sleep with one eye open, seed-muncher"

This is just a small sample of the daily tongue lashing I deliver to the foul beast. Sometimes I even get rude.

Bunny Smackin

I awoke this morning to a most horrific sight. Is it not enough that I have a squirrel living in my front yard? Now there is a bunny. No, not just any bunny, but a cute little fluffy, hippity-hoppity, nose wigglin, dandelion munchin, perky eared, little cotton tailed bunny. I never realized how quickly nausea can strike.

I suspect that Ivan has known of the bunnie's presence for some time. When I pointed the bunny out to him he feigned surprise, but Ivan is a poor actor. In retrospect, I fear that perhaps Ivan may have even been concealing the bunnie's presence. This smells of mutiny.

Intolerable. I decided to approach Tiger Lily about my suspicions. She of course whined, but in a guilty manner. What power does this hairy little hunk of hawk bait have over my minions? And more importantly, how can I steal it and use it for my own benefit?

This warrants more study.

In the meantime, both Ivan and Tiger Lily know that I suspect something. They do not know how much I know or how much I simply suspect and this makes them very nervous.

This amuses me.

For now, I wait. The bunny will give up it's secret someday. After I have learned the power of the bunny, I will have no more use for it. On that day I will deliver the bunny smack heard around the world.

B.O.B. (Big Overdecorated Bird)

While surveying my yard from my bedroom window, I observed something that truly irritated me.

Bob was on my back deck. For those of you who don't know who Bob is, allow me to describe him:

Bob is a huge bird thingy of what the two leggers call the peacock variety. This description I believe to be inaccurate. While I understand the second part of this label, the "pea" part escapes me. I can only surmise that it refers to his brain.

He is at least six tailspans in length and 3 tailspans tall. His plumage, well let's just say that he is an avian drag queen. He struts through my yard like he owns the place. The two leggers don't seem to mind. Absolutely unacceptable.

Now to be brutally honest, given our relative sizes, I was intimidated at first. But after further contemplation, I realized that he was several links further south on the food chain than I.

The food chain I speak of is as follows:

1) Me
2) Other felines
3) two leggers (if they amuse me)
4) other four leggers
5) catnip mousie thingies
6) birds
7) dust bunnies
8) anything having six or more legs.
9) squirrels

Therefore, like the front yard squirrel, Bob lives on borrowed time. For now, I wait. I am patient. However someday the two leggers will grow careless and leave a window or door open. On that blessed day, the yard will become a site of mass destruction and the following night I will sleep on a cushion made of squirrel fur and stuffed with beautiful feathers.

Utter Coon-fusion

I have discovered a new type of four legger. I am amused.

Last night, while on dust bunny patrol, I was startled by a loud skittering noise emanating from the back deck of my house. Assuming it was my nemesis the squirrel, I decided to aggressively ignore him. But the noise continued and eventually grew until it could be ignored no more. I stalked to the sliding door prepared to give the tree rat a glaring he wouldn't soon forget and to my dismay discovered that the squirrel was absent.

Instead, I beheld a large furry mound of mischief, and its' five mini-mounds.

Having spent much time watching Animal Planet on the talking box thingy, I quickly identified these trespassers as "raccoons". For those of you that have never actually seen a raccoon, they are about three tailspans long and weigh approximately two Ivans. They have grayish unkempt fur and black and white rings on their tails. They wear a mask on their face. I believe they are basically well dressed possums.

I decided to observe.

The large raccoon used its' incredibly dexterous paws to open the container of bird seed and sate itself on the contents therein. Meanwhile, the mini-coons were busy. Two of them were swimming in the koi pond, while the other three were dissecting the cushions of the lawn furniture. Occasionally two or more would suddenly begin to wrestle, hissing and biting at each other until they found other objects to explore and ultimately destroy. I have never witnessed such concentrated chaos. My heart pounded as I considered the possibilities.

Imagine these maestros of mayhem released upon the interior of my home. If they can cause such damage to furnishings designed to stand up to Mother Nature, what could they do to the all the delicate little thingies that my female two legger takes such pride in? Ivan would have new friends that smell almost as bad as him. The garbage can would never be upright again. Never again would I have to struggle with trying to bite through the lid of the catnip container. I bet that houseplants would never be seen in my house again. Just the thought of those guys lining up to smack Tiger Lily with their marvelous little paws makes me shiver in anticipation.

MWAHAHAHA!!!

I have made a decision. I am now their leader, and they are my minions.

Mutt-erings

I don't understand it.

I am confused.

I am annoyed because I don't understand it and it confuses me.

Why are dogs always so happy?

Between naps, snacks, litter box visits, slapping Tiger Lily and chaos creation, I have been pondering this very question.

What the hell is it that makes dogs so eternally happy?

They are happy when they see a two legger. They are happy when they don't see a two legger. They are happy when they are well fed. They are happy when they are hungry. They are happy when they are thrown a ball. They are happy when you only fake throwing them a ball. They are happy when they go poo, and then they are happy eating the poo that just made them happy when they left it. They are even happy when they are unconscious. They can be completely comatose and that tail will still be wagging.

My first thought was that their happiness stemmed from their lack of mental capacity. However, Ivan disproves this theory. He has the IQ of a mentally challenged dust bunny, yet he is very seldom happy. So obviously stupidity is not the key to a cheerful disposition. (Washington DC. would replace Disneyland as the "Happiest Place on Earth" otherwise.)

My second hypothesis involved a recreational drug that affects only canines. After searching the internet thingy, I failed to find any references to "dognip". I did however find several website thingies that discussed canine fashion, although the pictures seemed to have very little in common with "doggy style" and only confused me more.

My final consideration is that canine anatomy includes a "happy gland". I believe this gland is located in the dog's hindquarters. It is triggered by the dog's nose. Apparently there is a complimentary gland on the dog's nose that triggers the "happy gland" on the dog's butt.

Whenever a dog's nose comes into close contact with either its' own butt or that of another canine, some type of chemical reaction thingy takes place in the doggy brain that makes it incredibly happy. This reaction seems to be very short-lived causing the dog to constantly repeat the process, usually several hundred times per day.

Yes, this must be the answer.

Just a note to Cesar Millan.(The Dog Whisperer) If you require any more advice, I am at your service.

Canine Conundrum

Mimi, a four legger related to me by two legger marriage, (her two legger married the offspring of my two leggers) wrote to me with a dilemma. She writes:

"Dear Great and Powerful Cujo Cat,

My two legger recently got a dog. I know, terrible isn't it. It's a complete disaster! How could she let a stupid lumbering beast into my sacred territory (however small it is)? This dog is very unaware of its tail, (even though I don't see how any animal can be unaware of its tail) and smacks it around everywhere! It has come close to smacking me in the face, trampling me, stealing my food, and my two legger's attention when she should be paying attention to me! When she's looking, I act like I don't care but you gotta help me Cujo Cat! How do I get rid of this dog or at least put it in its rightful place?"

Mimi, there are several solutions to your situation. Please feel free to utilize the method best suited for you:

1) Find an electrical socket that is within easy reach of the offending mutt. Very carefully smear a dab of peanut butter over the outlet. Sit back and watch the sparks fly. If you can find butt flavored peanut butter, so much the better.
2) Bury several chunks of Ex-Lax in your litter box. No dog can resist raiding an unattended litter box for "kitty roca". Within a couple of hours the dog in question will have made such a mess, the two leggers will decide to banish it permanently to the yard.
3) Hire yourself an Ivan. He'll make the mongrel an offer he can't refuse.

4) Sprinkle small bits of black pepper on the pillows of the two leggers while they sleep. After a few sleepless nights of sneezing, they will be convinced they are allergic to dogs and will subsequently send the dog back to whence it came.

Finally, if all else fails, break everything within the dogs reach. Make sure the two leggers are out of the room when you do, and as always LEAVE NO WITNESSES.

I hope I have been of service. Please let me know how it works out. I almost envy you this opportunity for chaos.

D.O.G.
(Dopey Over-enthusiastic Gasbags)

While relaxing in the 11 o'clock bay window sunbeam, I observed a four legger of the canine variety approaching my abode. The temerity of this 25 lb. slobber source left me aghast. Did he not realize that he was treading upon my sacred territory? I have never actually been outside, but if I can see it, it is legally my territory. Allow me to tell you about dogs:

Dogs have no apparent right to exist. They are dirty. They don't cover their own fecal matter. They are clumsy. They obey the two leggers. (sell outs) They have no dignity whatsoever. Worst of all, they are loyal. Any one of these offenses would disqualify one from ever being a card carrying cat.

Dogs come in almost every shape and size. From the huge lumbering ones that leave a path of destruction in their wake, to the little bitty bug-eyed ones that spend all day shaking like rat shaped mounds of Jello.

And what's the deal with dogs and bones? Once we cats have killed something, we either eat it, put it in the shoes of the female two legger, or place it on their bed as a warning of our lethality. We do not take a piece of our victim, carry it around and gnaw on it at our leisure.

There is a word for that: Evidence.

When a dog-owning two legger returns home, he is greeted at the door with a tail wagging, saliva flinging, barking ball of idiocy. This gives the two legger an over-inflated sense of worth.

We cats however totally ignore our two leggers unless there is food involved. We may look at them when they enter, but if they are expecting a greeting, they shoulda bought a dog.

Finally let me make one last observation:

A female cat with babies is called a "Queen". Guess what they call a female dog with babies. I rest my case.

Well, lucky for him, the dog has now left my jurisdiction. If he only knew how close he came to feeling my wrath.

Don't Worry, Be Yappy

I am NOT amused.

The two leggers invited a couple of their friends to my house today. As if this wasn't bad enough, the visiting two leggers had the temerity to bring along their sad excuse for a canine. Allow me to elaborate:

This canine is of the "tea cup poodle" variety. Apparently "tea cup" poodles are tiny little versions of a larger form of mutt. It is approximately one tailspan in length and the same in height. It's eyes are buggy and it's only purpose in life seems to be standing on its' two leggers lap, yapping at the top of its' tiny little lungs while shaking like Richard Simmons at a biker rally. Its' name is "Kirby" but I prefer to call it "Smackbait". It is white and according to Ivan, tastes like chicken.

Upon the arrival of this little taste of purgatory, my two leggers informed me that they expected me to be nice. Funny how they can spend so much time with me and yet know so little about my personality. Curious. I assured them that I'd be happy to "play" with the tiny interloper. I have lots of games that I'm sure would be entertaining. For instance:

> Hide The Tiny Body
> Buggy Eyed Smackdown
> Tag Team Poodle Stomp
> Slap Everything That Shakes.
> Name That Blood Stain

Ivan and I finally decided to play a new game. We called it "Name That Sound". Come to find out, a vase dropped on a mini-mutt's head from a height of six tailspans actually makes a "tonk" sound. I coulda sworn it'd be more like "thunk". Who knew?

Well, the good news is that the dog is no longer shaking.

The Stranger

I am miffed. I am annoyed. Angry, irritated, P.O.'ed, and furthermore agitated. One could almost say that I am upset. Now, you folks all know how slow to anger and easy going I am, so to say that something has gotten under my skin must come as a mental head smack for you. What has got my hairballs in a bunch?

A stray.

Not just some poor little waif of a vagabond kitty searching for handouts at the gates of my kingdom, but a true feral, bad attitude, bunny munchin, bird stalking, squirrel lover. `

One morning, shortly after consuming my breakfast and giving Tiger Lily her "top o' the mornin to ye" smack, I happened to glance out the sliding door and beheld the largest feline I had ever seen. This thing was not just big, it was like something that one sees munching Tokyo on the talking box thingy. It had the same markings as Ivan, but was much poofier. Paws the size of my food bowl and the mangiest coat seen this side of Kmart. Its' tail had seen better days and I only counted three teeth when it yawned.

My first reaction was to go get Ivan. I considered Ivan, being the big dumb brute that he is, to be better equipped to handle this interloper. However, when Ivan looked out of the window, he mistakenly took the stranger to be his own reflection and immediately grabbed his stash of catnip and flushed it down the toilet.

I was left no choice but to deal with the trespasser myself.

I arched my back in the "Halloween cat" position. I poofed. I twitched my incredible tail. I bared my perfect and complete set of teeth. I hissed and cursed and questioned his lineage. I even told him that he smelled of dog.

It is unfortunate that the two leggers installed insulated windows last year because the stranger was completely unaware of the superior tongue lashing he was receiving.

Finally, out of frustration, I body slammed Tiger Lily into the window causing her cry in her whiny, glass penetrating voice. This annoyed the stranger so much that he left for greener (and less irritating) pastures.

This was of course my strategy all along.

Resolution Revolution

Two leggers have an incredibly annoying habit.

Ok, that's a little too non-specific.

AMONG the two legger's incredibly annoying habits, is one that they perform once a year like clockwork. Once a year, every year, right after Christmas, they engage in the most annoying behavior of all.

They dwell in self analysis. They look back on the previous twelve months and try to figure out what they have been doing wrong. They look at all the things that have gone awry in their lives. They forensically examine all the minutiae that make up the crime scene of their psyche.

Then in a burst of ill advised self-improvement, they set out to change EVERYTHING.

Yup, everything.

At once.

They do not emulate Mother Nature with her slow, patient and eternally wise method of slowly sculpting the landscape, one pebble at a time. Turning a creek into a stream, a stream into a river, a river into a torrent over an expanse of time.

They jump right on their bulldozer thingy and start figuratively breaking mountains and scalping forests.

They have to quit nasty habits, lose weight and start giving more to charity. They must get more organized, clean the uncleanable closet and start going to church again.

Before February.

All two leggers have in their genetic makeup an annual alarm clock thingy. This alarm clock thingy goes off without exception on the Second of February every year. It signals the demise of every promise that the two leggers make on the First of January. If the goal has not been met when the alarm thingy goes off, the two leggers mutter a collective "screw it" and await their next bout of self analysis.

Silly and self-defeating if you ask me.

Two leggers should (as always) take a lesson from us feline types.

Say "Screw it" on the First of January.

We do not dwell on what is wrong in our world. We dwell on what is RIGHT in our world.

"I've put on a coupla pounds this year" This means I was well fed.

"I didn't go to Church this Sunday" I said my prayers Saturday and slept in on Sunday.

"I didn't eat healthy food" I ate food that tasted good.

Now I'm not saying two leggers should not give more to charity, this is an activity that I happen to agree with.

Please have your two leggers send their donations to:

 www.cujoneedsmorecatnip.com

Thank you for your support.

I guarantee it will go to a good cause.

Rain Blows

It is raining today. Why is this noteworthy? Because it irritated me. Why did it irritate me? Read on, McDuff.

As a rule, rain seldom irritates me. It occasionally even amuses me. When it rains, it will sometimes irritate the two leggers. They often plan outdoor activities only to have them ruined by rain. Given our geographic location, one would think that they would never plan anything that takes place outdoors. But being the incurable optimists that they are, (which I find unbearably irritating) they go ahead and plan away. Therefore when Mother Nature reaches out and smacks their plans into soggy oblivion, it amuses me.

It also amuses me when it rains because I am fully aware that the neighbor's yappy little shiver hound is stuck outside until his two leggers return from work. I enjoy sitting in the bay window, observing him sitting on his front porch shaking like, well, one of those really shaky thingies. I have even been known to chortle at this.

The reason the rain annoyed me today was the fact that the two leggers were home all day with nothing in particular planned. This compelled them to declare a "lazy day". In essence, they sat around all day with nothing to do but impede my activities. Every time I decided to torture Tiger Lily, the male would grab the water squirty thingy and chase me into the spare room until the urge had passed. I was unable to cause any damage because they were ALWAYS watching. Ivan spent the whole day on the female's lap so I was unable to mess with him. I couldn't even bird watch because apparently the bird thingies took a "lazy day" as well.

Finally I have reached a decision. I will nap. It won't amuse me, however it will have the benefit of allowing me to stay up ALL night sowing hate and discontent. They may have had a "lazy day", but their night should be somewhat more interesting.

Reign of The Rain

Honestly, how much water can there possibly be in the sky?

I am fully aware that I reside in the Great Northwest. I know that the Great Northwest is known for its' prodigious annual rainfall.

But, who do I have to smack to get a sunbeam?

It has been raining everyday for the last bajillion days.

Everything is wet. I don't do wet. Wet is what happens when the two leggers get annoyed and chase me with the water squirty thingy. Wet is what happens when Ivan forgets that two leggers just put water in the tub thingy. Wet is what happens when I knock over a glass that the two leggers neglected to take to the kitchen. (Ok, that last one is somewhat amusing, but you get my point.)

If there was a bright side, I may try to gaze upon it. But, there is no bright side!

IT'S RAINING!

Everything is dark and dismal.

However, this eternal deluge does have a few amusing aspects.

For instance: It confuses Ivan. Whenever I notice that Ivan has found a comfy spot and settled down for a power nap, I jump onto a windowsill and yell "Sweet! Sunbeam!" Ivan knocks over furniture in his misguided attempt to enjoy a solar nap. Of course, as soon as he reaches the window, I tell him in a sympathetic voice "Sorry old buddy, you just missed it."

The truly sad thing is that he even falls for this ruse at night.

Tiger Lily is naturally whining about the rain. I'd smack her, but I think she would welcome the pain as a relief from the monotony.

There is one silver lining to the cloud upon cloud outside my window.

That silver lining naturally involves the indigenous squirrel population. As miserable as it is to sit and watch the rain from my window day after day, I know in my little feline heart that the squirrels have it worse. Sitting in their soaked, dirty little nests, not a single mangy, hair un-matted. Given the fact that raincoats do not come in nasty little vermin sizes, they must be beyond miserable.

Wow, I feel much better now. Think I'll go make Tiger Lily's day.

Spring Fevered

Springtime in the Pacific Northwest is barely discernible from the other three seasons in the Pacific Northwest. It is rainy, cold, windy and generally foul outside.

So how can I tell when Spring has arrived?

Easy.

Not only is it foul outside, but there are *fowl* outside.

That's right, the bird thingies are returning. This requires my constant attention. I feel compelled to stand vigil at the windows and doors of my house.

The bird thingies must be watched. I'm not sure why, I only know that they must be watched.

Bird thingies come in many different shapes and sizes. From the itty bitty yellow and black ones, to the unnaturally large ones with the black and brown bodies and white heads. The smaller bird thingies feed on seeds and nuts that the two leggers provide, while the larger ones seem to feed on the smaller bird thingies. I respect this. The carnage amuses me.

The exception to this size equals appetite theory is Bob. He eats grapes and other things that don't bleed. He annoys me.

The smaller bird thingies are much more prevalent. They spend their day flitting about from branch to branch, eating seeds, chirping, tweeting and using the lawn furniture as their litter box. Aside from being a protein source, their purpose eludes me.

The other major symptom of Spring: Squirrel thingies. Alas, my hopes that the wind, snow and bitter temperatures that wreaked havoc on the yard may have decimated the squirrel infestation, have gone unrewarded. They are back, dancing on the deck, playing in my yard, and being unreasonably cheerful. There is nothing in my world that annoys me more.

It is my belief that the bird thingies consort with squirrel thingies. They both live in trees, they eat seeds and nuts, they always seem happy.

They all must die.

Unfortunately, it is not within my power to erase their enthusiasm. The windows have proven themselves to be beyond my breakage capabilities. So every morning, Ivan and I sit in our windows and watch. We chitter. We occasionally growl. We have even been known to hiss.

But mostly we watch.

We wait in tail twitching anticipation for The Day. The Day when the two leggers carelessly leave a window open and the wrath of Cujo is unleashed upon all the feathered and mangy furred denizens of my yard.

Ivan's wrath will also be released, but it will be directed at the rose bush. I don't know why, and Ivan does not wish to talk about it.

The Prodigal Sun Returns

I would like to welcome back an old friend.

Yes, after being away for the last seven months, my sunbeam has returned.

Oh, how I have missed it.

For some as yet unexplained reason, my sunbeam disappears in September, and then refuses to return until April or May. This truly annoys me.

I suspect it migrates south for the winter.

But all is well now. I woke up yesterday and spotted it sitting in my bay window, acting very aloof, as though it had never abandoned me. Silently, so as to not alert the other felines, I stalked the sunbeam. I was extremely careful not to spook it because sunbeams in my neck of the woods are extraordinarily skittish and tend to flee if caution is not exercised.

I crept in a low crouch, senses on high alert for the approach of Ivan and Tiger Lily lest they attempt to claim the prey for themselves. Once I deemed myself within pouncing range, I leapt, landing full straddle upon the unsuspecting ray, pinning it to the sill, totally at my mercy.

Satisfied that the beam was subdued, I began my ritualistic sunbeam yoga. Sunbeam yoga is an ancient feline form of exercise that consists of several very difficult pose thingies. I have, of course, mastered them all. Allow me to describe just a few of these:

Sprawled Dead Mousie—One lays on their back, chin jutting and legs parallel to the windowsill.

Creepy Pretzel—Once again, laying prone, but with legs akimbo, one paw wrapped around the head, eyes closed and teeth bared.

Crackhead Sphinx—Sitting on ones brisket, forepaws tucked, wild manic look while chittering. This pose thingy is especially good for watching bird thingies.

Joy To The Swirled—Laying on one's side, forming a perfect circle, connecting nose to tail.

There are many more pose thingies, but they all have one common denominator: If performed by a master such as myself, they can lead to total relaxation and productive napping.

Now, I am afraid that I must return to my bay window to continue my routine before Ivan wakes up and harshes my mellow.

Easter Greetings

As has become my holiday tradition, I have decided to torture my followers with a bit of poetry. Thus I present my Easter poem. Enjoy.

This weekend it is Easter,
And I find it sort of funny.
Everyone making such a fuss,
Over an egg laying little bunny.

The two leggers have been busy,
Cooking quite the feast.
All for a long eared, long legged,
Annoying little beast.

They have cleaned my house, they have mown the lawn,
They have even swept the floor.
They made little decorations,
To hang upon the door.

I suppose they'll have guests come,
And invade my happy home.
And all through my private spaces,
The two leggers, they will roam.

They'll pat me, they'll pet me,
They'll say "Who's the little kitty?"
When I leave them bleeding,
I will show them little pity.

I do not understand,
This springtime holiday.
But if they insist on this madness,
I promise they will pay.

Just what is this Easter?
What's it all about?
I sat and pondered this,
And before long figured out.

It's not about the bunny,
The puddings or the hams.
It's not about the colored eggs,
Or the dish of candied yams.

It's about something different,
To you, this idea I toss.
It's supposed to be about,
That two legger on the cross.

It seems he died for us,
And then was born again.
He went through all of that,
So we'd be free of sin.

He gave up his life on Earth,
So that we would all be freed.
And trust me, with my record,
Forgiveness, I will need.

Oh, I'll still watch my yard,
Watching is my habit.
And even if it's sinful,
I will munch that Easter Rabbit.

Mother's Day Ponderings

There is one day each year that the two leggers set aside to honor their mothers. In their usual lack of imagination, they have deemed it "Mother's Day"

Now, in my house, all the spawn of my two leggers have either been taken to the shelter, or adopted by other felines. Other than for occasional visits, they are seldom seen in my kingdom. Therefore, I have little experience in what may or may not constitute a good "mother".

And so I find myself pondering this question.

Since I adopted the Dunn's when I was only twelve weeks old, I have few memories of my own mother, but those few are quite vivid.

Basically, she was a lunatic.

Not the "cute and funny, sitting in the corner talking to shadows, listening to the voices tell her that the key to world peace relies on her bread tie collection" sort of lunatic.

I'm talking the "scary, makes you sleep with one eye open, hide the sharp utensils, never make eye contact, psycho-nut" variety of lunatic.

I recall one instance when, after my siblings and I had just finished nursing, she suddenly jumped up and announced that she had replaced her milk with goat milk and that we would all have horns by morning. She then proceeded to rub her butt on the carpet while laughing maniacally.

Another time, she informed us that we had been harvested too young and attempted to "re-plant" us in the litterbox thingy.

Every time she saw her own reflection in a mirror, she would spontaneously start quoting lines from "Chitty Chitty Bang Bang".

It is my firm belief that she did a LOT of catnip in her younger days.

Back to the present day.

After pondering "mothers", I have reached the conclusion that my female two legger must be a pretty good one.

She has raised her young in a loving environment. (not really my thing, but to each their own) While giving sound advice and guidance, she has always let them choose their own paths and make their own mistakes. She has always celebrated their successes, while never belaboring their failures.

I consider these actions to be the hallmark of good "mothering". This also explains why her offspring hold her in such high regard.

Just a final note. My male two legger is afraid that some of my readers may infer that when I spoke of my own mother, I may have also been casting aspersions upon his mother.

I assure you that this may or may not be true.

A History Lesson

The fourth day of July.

Every year on this date, the two leggers decide to celebrate by cooking their meal outside on my deck. They consume food and drink and socialize into the wee hours. Generally, fire and loud noises are involved.

I find this behavior curious.

So once again, I decided to ponder this two legged tradition. This is what I have discovered:

It seems that about 235 two legger years ago, (approximately 80.347 bajillion cat years) the two leggers that lived in North America decided that they no longer cared to be associated with the two leggers that lived across the ocean thingy. So they told them off and decided that from that day forth, they would be self-governing. (unless they had cats)

What many of you may be unaware of, is the fact that without cats, none of this would have been possible.

Back in 1776, the Founding Two Leggers were suffering under the oppression of being ruled by a government that took the fruit of their labors and gave them little in return. The British cared little for their American minions except as a source of food, catnip and reality television programs. The Americans one day woke up and said "We do not need a King thingy to eat our food, use our catnip, steal our ideas for television programming, and generally treat us like litter. We have cats!"

So a group of two leggers led by George Jefferson, Washington DeeCee, Old MacDonald and Bud Wiser wrote a nastygram to the Burger King and demanded a tea party. The Burger King was annoyed and sent some lobsters and a squid or two to America to show his displeasure.

This deployment of seafood did not impress the two leggers and annoyed their cats who were expecting tuna. So in a fit of pique, the two leggers wrote another nastygram called "The Declaration Bill of Independent Rights Constitutional Thingy". This really put the Burger King's Royal Pantaloons in a twist and so he sent more lobsters. I do not understand the British strategy of seafood warfare, but then again, they are British.

Long story short, the American two leggers shot and ate the all the lobsters that the British sent. Eventually the Burger King lost interest and started shipping his seafood elsewhere.

To this day, American two leggers celebrate the Fourth of July by eating hotdogs, hamburgers and apple pie.

Anything but lobster.

Fireside Cat

My favorite time of year has to be fire season. I love fire season. Here in my house it lasts about nine months. Not near long enough, but I have plans to lengthen it.

No, I'm not referring to the time of year when a whole bunch of wild tree thingies go up in flames, the season to which I refer occurs when the temperature gets low enough that the two leggers decide to turn on my firebox.

About the only thing the two leggers have that is worthy of my respect is their ability to instantly create fire. About three years ago, while I was still an adorable kitten (about six months before I became an adorable adult), the two leggers paid three hygiene challenged two leggers (they smelled of dog) to come into my house and build the great and wonderful firebox thingy. At first I was less than amused. They removed my favorite "sit and glare at the two leggers" table. Then over the course of seven hours, they banged, talked and annoyed me in general, causing me to miss at least three naps.

With no consideration of my royal presence, they brought in things that cut stuff, and things that put stuff back together. They failed to beg my permission, they failed to give me offerings. At one point, they even had the ineffable temerity to refer to me as a "bad little kitty" when I attempted to smack them into line.

Just when I thought I could take no more and was just about to send Ivan to mess them up, they packed up their things and left. They had replaced my favorite table with the firebox thingy.

At first I didn't like it at all. I still decided it was mine, but I didn't like it. It spans the entire distance between floor and ceiling and therefore I am unable sit atop it. This annoyed me. It is made of a very hard wood, therefore I am unable to scratch or damage it. Also very annoying.

I sat glaring at it until the two leggers returned home. They seemed inordinately happy about this new addition to my home. The male then picked up a tiny button box and "WHOOF", fire appeared. I saw that it was good.

I immediately made the two leggers place my throne in front of it and informed everyone that this belonged to me.

Ivan is of course confused by fire. I've tried to explain that fire makes heat, but complex theories like that are simply beyond his microbrain. I allow Tiger Lily to lay in front of it on occasion but only if it is off and I am napping elsewhere and thus unaware of her trespass.

Earlier, I spoke of extending the fire season. I have been carefully observing the way the two leggers light the firebox. I am positive that the little button box is the key in making fire. However I've yet to crack that nut. Whenever the two leggers leave, I experiment with the tiny button box. But so far all I have been able to do is activate the talking box thingy. But I do not despair.

It is only a matter of time and observation.

Someday I will discover their secret and all will sweat because of it.

Oktoberpest

Every October, two leggers have a tradition of making or purchasing Halloween costumes for us four legged types. This sits squarely on the "non-amusing" side of the ledger. Even if you allow for the scarcity of employed brain cells within the two leggers noggins, there is no possible way for them not to realize that this behavior does not amuse us. How can they honestly believe that we sit around all day, wishing that they would suddenly grab one of us and begin wrapping us in costumes that when finished, make us look like clowns that are about to mutilate anything that comes within reach? Then they pull out their camera thingy and take as many pictures as possible before someone loses an eye.

I can't even give them credit for originality. Take Ivan's costume for example: Let's think . . . . he's round, slightly striped, hollow headed and goofy looking. Ohhh! I know, let's dress him as a jack-o-lantern! Duh.

Tiger Lily does require a little imagination, but not much. She's gray, irritating, totally un-amusing and whines a lot, they put a necktie on her and call her David Letterman.

As for myself, I already wear a tuxedo 24/7 so they simply place me next to a martini glass and a pistol and call me "James Bond". Unfortunately the pistol thingy is not real, otherwise the only pictures being taken would be by those two leggers that wear the jackets that say "CSI".

Someday, when we finally put the two leggers on trial for crimes against feline dignity, these pictures will be exhibit A. The only sentence that could possibly rectify this vile injustice will be dressing them as four leggers and making them go out and spend hours among other two leggers.

Dang, they already do that.

Cats Your Fate To The Wind

As many of you know, I live in the Puget Sound region. The weather here during October is, shall we say, predictably unpredictable. Sometimes it is rainy. Sometimes it is windy. Sometimes it is windy and rainy. At other times, it is rainy and windy. It is often rainy and windy and rainy with wind. It has been known to be wet and blustery. Moist and blowing. Gusty and pouring. Sprinkly and gusty.

You get the idea. It just so happens that this weekend, we had wind and rain.

I spent the entire weekend watching a tree in the front yard. This may sound like a boring way to spend a weekend, but I have my reasons. Okay, really just one reason. I know the squirrel lives in that tree. I was awaiting his demise.

As soon as the windstorm struck, I began imagining the squirrel being blown out the tree, falling from the upper branches to a final meeting with Mother Earth. Perhaps he would scream or at least squeal all the way down. Perhaps he would realize in his final moments how incredibly irritating his constant, irrational optimism was to all other creatures in his vicinity and repent. I entertained a mental image of him falling and not dying right away, but instead suffering, while Ivan and I watched from our warm abode giggling, as his limbs slowly went numb.

Alas, my wish was not granted. Apparently the same claw thingies that enable him to scurry up and down the tree in the most annoyingly nimble manner also allow him to cling securely to said tree even in the highest winds. I am annoyed.

At the same time however, I am amused. I am amused because I can imagine how he spent the last seventy-two hours. Hanging on for dear life while the wind whips around his arboreal abode, the rain penetrating every millimeter of his flea bitten fur. My dearest wish is that he can see me from his precarious perch, sitting in my window, comfy, dry and totally unaffected by the wind.

It was not to be. The storm subsided this morning. The squirrel scurried out of his tree looking none the worse for wear. The storm also succeeded in knocking the rest of the pine cones out of the tree making the squirrels labor that much easier.

Sometimes I honestly believe that Mother Nature truly hates me.

Snow Wonder

What the hell happened to my yard?

I am confused. Yesterday, around 9 am, I settled down for my early mid-morning nap. I chose the front bay window as the spot because the sun was shining and therefore it was prime napping real estate. Gazing out at the green grass, I drifted off to sleep.

I was in the middle of a wonderful dream that involved a decapitated squirrel and a one winged bird (it kept flying in circles), when I was awakened by the sound of Ivan running through my house in full blown poofy fur, crooked tail, freakout mode. Now, it doesn't take much to freak out Ivan (simply asking him where his tail went usually accomplishes this) but this freakout seemed beyond the pale.

I opened my eyes slowly, working up to a major league tabby smack, and to my utter astonishment discovered that the entire outside world had changed. The sun was gone and everything was covered in big white flaky thingies (and I'm not referring to talk show hosts).

These big white flaky thingies (BWFT's) were falling from the sky at an enormous rate. They fell silently and slowly, threatening to lull me back to sleep. Fortunately my curiosity served to keep me awake so that I could ponder this oddity.

The first thing I noticed was the scarcity of any four leggers in the yard. Normally, the deck bunny is hopping around the front yard at this time of day. He was nowhere to be seen. No bird thingies were in evidence. Even the stupid squirrel was missing. The only four leggers I could see were the goats. They were standing in their shed, clearly displeased, glaring at the house as though this was somehow my doing.

Ivan kept running from window to window trying to capture some of the BWFT's with no success. (Like so many other concepts, Ivan doesn't understand glass) Tiger Lily whined for a while and then curled up on a hot air vent and fell asleep. I'll smack her after I solve this mystery.

Shortly thereafter, the two leggers came home early. To my delight, some of the BWFT's had stuck to the female's boots. I waited while she removed her boots and left them by the door. After she left the room, I was able to examine the BWFT's more closely.

Upon close examination, (sniffing and batting) I discovered that the BWFT's were:

A. Cold
B. Wet
C. Very cold
D. Very Cold and wet.

The only flavor I could discern was leather, presumably from the female's boots.

My conclusion is that the BWFT's are water that has been transformed into a sticky, goat irritating substance.

The male two legger turned on the talking box thingy and watched another two legger talk about a "snow" storm. I soon realized that he was referring to the BWFT's. Best of all, the BWFT's were causing much chaos in two legged society. He spoke of cars in ditches, businesses and schools closing, and roads being blocked. I watched for some time hoping to hear about squirrel casualties, but none were reported. Perhaps they'll find their mangy little corpses after the BWFT's melt. One can only hope.

BWFT= snow. Mystery solved.

After much consideration, I have decided that I must learn how to manufacture this stuff.

The Best Time of The Year

I am giddy. I am beside myself with anticipation. My favorite season has arrived.

Every year when the weather grows cold, the trees lose their leaves and the wind blows the squirrel around the yard, my two legged minions suddenly feel the urge to fill my abode with a wide array of cat toys. There are toys of every shape and size.

My personal favorite is a miniature tree thingy that stretches from floor to ceiling. Not only do they conveniently place it in the middle of my living room, they also hang a myriad of dangly, shiny, sparkly and crunchy objects from the branches. Some are even quite delicious. These objects are perfectly tailored for feline amusement. There are colored round balls hanging from small hooks that are made to shatter on impact. They make a very satisfying popping sound when they drop.

The tree thingy also makes an incredibly effective ambush site. Tiger Lily has yet to learn that the tree thingy has an unlimited supply of smacks lurking within its verdant boughs. I spend most of my day carefully climbing among the branches, looking for the best position from which to observe and plot. I have learned from past experience to be utterly still whenever a two legger enters so that I don't alert them to my intentions. I like for them to be surprised when I leap at them from the upper branches. It enhances the enjoyment for all involved.

Ivan, on the other hand, likes the tree thingy for the variety of flavors that it contains. He seems to enjoy the taste of plastic and cotton. I don't claim to understand him, he is what he is. He especially enjoys chewing the wires that connect the tiny lightbulbs. Occasionally while chewing on these, he will suddenly jump straight up and flee from the room leaving only the smell of singed fur behind. One would think this to be an unpleasant experience, but ten minutes later he'll be back contentedly munching away.

There are ribbons, bows, boxes wrapped in thin paper, all easily shredded and destroyed. Every night, we wreak havoc and destruction. Every morning the two leggers spend an hour or so resetting everything and sweeping up the shards while screaming in joy and amusement.

Christmas Un-decoration

I feel inspired to write another poem:

Twas three days till Christmas,
And all round the tree,
Something was lurking.
That something was me.

The presents were shredded,
Torn up with great care.
The stockings were torn,
And covered with hair.

Ornaments were shattered,
Shards on the floor,
The star at the top,
Will twinkle no more.

The light thingies were pretty,
Until they were snagged.
And then down the hallway,
They were tastefully dragged.

The angel stood gracefully.
Appearing to sing,
Until Ivan smacked her,
And tore off a wing.

Then to the Wise Men,
Standing next to the manger,
The camels and sheep,
Were subject to danger.

The mini Santa and presents.
Lay ruined in heaps,
Then we munched Rudolph,
And a few of his "peeps".

Now is the time,
To await with great glee,
The two legger's reaction,
To the demise of their tree.

A Christmas Tail

Twas the night before Christmas,
And all through my house,
Came the thump, thump, thumping,
Of Ivan punching a mouse.

The two leggers were sleeping,
All snug in their beds.
Oblivious to the world,
They had taken their meds.

I lay on my throne,
And started to snooze.
I dreamed of smacking squirrels,
And barfing in shoes.

Suddenly something woke me,
A noise on the roof.
Yanking me from slumber
Causing me to poof.

Standing by the firebox,
What did I behold?
A big fat two legger,
Who looked rather old.

He was big, fat and bearded.
He was dressed all in red.
I ordered Mr. Ivan,
To bring me his head.

But, Ivan refused.
He wouldn't even budge.
Because Ivan suspected,
This guy carried fudge.

Ivan begged me to chill,
As I reached for a stick,
"This bozo is none other,
Than good ole St. Nick."

Ivan's determination,
Caused me to pause.
Could this obese vagrant,
Be Santa Claus?

He gives people presents,
He is a merry soul.
But all he ever brings for me,
Is a big old lump of coal.

And so I swore, then and there,
By my jingle balls.
Next time I see him,
I'm giving Santa claws.

Christmas Greetings

Twas the day of Christmas,
And all through my spaces,
The two leggers were laughing,
And stuffing their faces.

They all seem so happy,
So sated with bliss.
Something is wrong,
Something's amiss.

We've been working so hard,
Ivan and I,
To Cause chaos and mayhem,
And make two leggers cry.

It just isn't right,
It doesn't seem fair.
Instead of angst and strife,
There's joy in the air.

We've shredded the tree.
We've broken the lights.
Even the shepherds know,
The pain of our bites.

But early this morning,
As I lay gently sleeping,
That fat two legger in red,
Into my house came creeping.

At the exact same moment,
We spotted each other.
I saw him go pale, he started to shudder.

"Oh no, not you!"
He screamed out in fright,
This had just become,
The last stop of the night.

He threw his bag at the tree,
He dived for his sleigh.
Ivan was too slow,
The bozo got away.

"See you next year!",
I yelled to the night.
But the only response I heard,
Was a shaky "Yeah, right."

And so the two leggers,
Have had their holiday.
While Ivan and I sulk,
And put hairballs in their way.

But we'll get over it,
You need never fear.
We've caused a lot of damage,
Plus. there's always next year.

Return of The BWFTs

Once again, my yard has gone AWOL.

For the last two days BWFTs have been falling.

This time the BWFTs are much larger and numerous than before. They completely cover my yard and all the various thingies therein.

I am unsure whether to be amused or annoyed.

I am somewhat amused because I imagine that the squirrel thingy is suffering terribly. Freezing his little acorns off, his mangy tail caked with ice and slush. I know that at the very least, he is very uncomfortable and irritated with Mother Nature. I keep hoping that the two leggers will pity him and allow him to come inside. This will allow me to "educate" him on his place in the local food chain. I have tried to convince them that I would not harm the little pest . . . . uhm, I mean cutie, but I'm afraid they have serious misgivings about my intentions.

Their mistrust annoys me.

The BWFTs also annoy because they have revealed another type of pestilence infecting my yard. Last night, I noticed several lights emanating from beneath the snow.

My female two legger informed me that these were "gnome houses". I have heard of these gnome thingies, but had never imagined that they lived in houses or that they would have the temerity to build a development in my yard.

From what I have gathered, gnomes are miniature two leggers with pointed heads and annoying voices with British accents. This is unacceptable. I do not wish to see them in my yard. They require immediate eviction.

I am unsure what they feed on, but they if they are expecting to freeload on my property, they are sadly mistaken. The two leggers seem unfazed by them, but Ivan and I are most annoyed. As soon as I spot one, I intend to give him a tongue lashing he won't soon forget.

And so I turn to my loyal readers. If anyone out there has any experience in dealing with or eradicating gnome thingies, please let me know.

Unless they eat squirrels.

Compete Fools

Today I did some pondering.

I know that many of you will say: "But Cujo, you are always pondering!"

Today I was doing some truly deep pondering

No, not "What is the meaning of life in the universe?" type pondering. I've already cracked that nut thingy.

But deep pondering none the less.

I was pondering the compulsion that two leggers have to compete with one another.

Anyone who has spent any time at all watching the talking box thingy has surely noticed that the majority of mindless programs involve some type of competition. Two leggers do not seem happy unless they are showing that they are better at something than other two leggers.

They compete in contests to find out who is better at thinking, running, singing, dancing, cheating, unsound decision making, cooking, eating, fighting and hitting a small white ball around a park, just to name a few.

At any given time, I am sure that half of the two legged population is busy attempting to prove their competitive prowess while the other half is watching them at home on their talking box thingies.

Sometimes they compete individually, sometimes in pairs, packs or teams.

I find this curious. I suppose they must get something out of it. I know they are usually rewarded with money or trophy thingies. But being a cat, I have no use for these things. Oh sure, I am aware that money buys catnip, and I know from experience that trophies make a satisfying sound when knocked off a high shelf, but still the logic escapes me.

It cannot be the hope that the rest of two legged society is going to remember them throughout eternity. The "Champions" are invariably forgotten as soon as the next competition begins. (Unless they are caught in a drug scandal and then their fame lasts somewhat longer, but not much)

It cannot be for establishing dominance or authority, the two leggers spend a full year "electing" their leaders and then the next three years grumping about how bad they are.

Once again, two leggers should learn from their feline superiors. The only reason to compete is for fun.

My definition of fun is as follows:

1. Anything that causes discomfort in others.
2. Anything that causes major structural damage.
3. Anything that makes a two legger jump from their bed at 3 a.m. and run screaming in elation through my house spraying the water squirty thingy at anything that moves. (preferably Tiger Lily)
4. Anything that causes Tiger Lily to whine.
5. Ritual Squirrel sacrifice.

As far as competition for dominance or authority, we simply smack each other around until someone hides under the entertainment center. Or until Tiger Lily whines and we end up declaring a tie and spend the rest of the evening smacking her.

Field of Snores

The male two legger is excited. This annoys me. What has him so excited? Baseball. Apparently "his" team is doing well. The success of his team causes him to jump and shout at unexpected intervals. Since I don't understand two legger sports, I decided to first observe, and then if I deem it worthy, suggest improvements.

When I first heard the two leggers discussing baseball, I actually found myself becoming interested. They spoke of bats, flies, balls, running home, and most intriguing of all: "fowl balls". I thought it might be some sort of culinary competition. However, I was mistaken.

After careful observation of a game on the talking box thingy, I can safely say that two leggers who watch sports develop a completely different lexicon. For instance:

Bat—A large wooden club, not a flying mousie thingie.

Balls—Ok, they are pretty much round objects, made to be thrown and chased. However, it also means a poorly thrown, ... well . . . . ball.

Running home—No, they don't leave the park and go to their house, they run between four white things, returning to the white thing they started at. Very confusing.

Fowl balls—Well, I totally misunderstood both the meaning and spelling of this term. Apparently avian anatomy has nothing to do with this sport. (See also "Fly balls")

Now to say that the logic of this sport escapes me would be a massive understatement. At first glance it appeared that the man holding the ball (or pitcher) was trying to hit the guy holding the bat. (batter) The batter then attempts to fend off the ball with the big wooden club while simultaneously trying to drive the ball back at one of the two leggers standing behind the pitcher. After hitting the ball, the batter then drops the bat and runs to one of the white things as the other two leggers try to tag him with the ball. (If he just kept the bat with him, I bet the other two leggers would stop trying to tag him.)

However, upon further observation, I realized that the pitcher was actually trying to miss the batter, but only by a little bit. And the batter was actually trying to hit the ball AWAY from the other players. After watching for about a half hour, I realized that there would be little or no bloodshed involved and decided that somewhere there was paint drying that was in need of watching.

Other than allowing all the players to carry bats at all times, I have no suggestions for making this sport more interesting.

In short, I've come to this realization about two leggers: Two legger sports are nothing but excuses to shirk their duties and drink beer. I guarantee that if they televised me stalking and slapping Tiger Lily, some two legged male would grab a six pack, forget his lawn, and spend four hours a day on a couch yelling about how in his day he coulda slapped her better.

Perhaps they'll give me my own channel.

Field of Snores (Revisited)

I thought that Baseball Season in my house would have ended by now. I was mistaken. It has not only continued, it has gained in intensity. Non-amusing in the extreme.

It would appear that my male two leggers favorite team refuses to stop playing. In all previous years, they have quit playing by mid September and the male two legger has restricted his yelling at the talking box thingy to Sundays when he watches football. But this baseball playoff madness seems to have no end.

Apparently his team, the Rangers, are competing with the Giants in The World Series. I have heard that the winners of this competition get to wear special jewelry and then go visit a six foot tall talking mouse thingy named "Mickey". Big deal.

However, something puzzles me. Where do the two leggers come up with the names of their teams? I have pondered this at length and have reached no satisfactory conclusions. Please allow me to explain my confusion:

The Giants: They do not appear monstrously large.
The Rangers: They do not seem to wander any more than the other teams.
The Mariner: They wear neither floppy hats nor eyepatches, however it seems that their ship has indeed sailed.
The Indians: They appear be to neither Native American nor Hindu.

And finally, The Yankees. This moniker is possibly the most confusing of all. It is my understanding that in order to have a "Yankee", there must first be a "Yanker" I do not understand how there can be the one without there being the other. So I took a poll. I inquired of of all the people that I know that follow baseball. Here are the results:

2% said that I misunderstood the term "Yankee" (Highly doubtful, and their shoes will pay later)
3% said they didn't know.
95 % said "Yankees" and "Yankers" are synonymous.

This greatly amused my two legger.

Messing With The Two Leggers

I had a MWAHAHAHA moment yesterday. Allow me to elaborate:

Last night, my female two legger left her diamond earring thingies out. I do not claim to understand why she holds these so dear, but I know they are among her prize possessions.

As soon as I realized she had left them out, I was deafened by the sound of opportunity knocking. I quickly grabbed one and hid it under the refrigerator. "Why only one?" you may ask, be patient, soon you will realize there is madness to my method. The other earring thingy I gave a shallow grave in the litter box.

I watched this morning as the male two legger scooped the litter. The look on his face when he discovered the partially buried earring thingy was priceless. Thus ensued the most thorough cleaning of my litter box that I have ever witnessed. I believe I can now boast of the cleanest litter in the pacific northwest.

Now, he cleans the litter box every time we go. It is quite amusing. Every time he hears scratching, he appears, wielding his litter scoop like Excalibur. He sifts the litter like a gold crazy forty-niner sifting his claim.

As a bonus, Ivan is one of those strange felines that feels the need to soil the litter after every cleaning. It's almost like a dance. The two legger scoops, Ivan squats, the two legger scoops, Ivan squats. Who will give in first? I'll have to make sure Ivan stays hydrated. It has been a truly amusing day.

However, I just realized a flaw in my evil plan, the two leggers read my writings.

Oh well, it was fun while it lasted. I'm sure they'll make me sleep with Ivan tonight, but it was worth it. I just hope they retrieve my catnip mousie thingy while they are under the fridge.

Wrassle-Mania 2011

A few days ago, the male two legger left the talking box thingy turned on while he worked in the yard. Shortly after he left, a show came on that attracted my attention.

The name of the show was "World's Most Extreme Mixed Martial Arts Tae Kwon Do Karate Jujitzu Kung Fu Ultimate Wrestling And Fighting Championship". (WMEMMATKDKJKFWFC, for short)

It was sponsored by The Peace Corps.

Anyway, I was fascinated by this program. Two leggers were busily slapping, kicking, punching, throwing things, choking and generally maiming each other. And nobody was spraying them with the water squirty thingy. In fact, other two leggers were cheering them on.

This could be the greatest thing I have ever seen on the talking box thingy.

Even better than "When Animals Attack".

It was then that it dawned on me.

We could sooooo do this.

First thing we needed was cool wrassling names.

Ivan became: "Ivan The Orange Crusher"

We named Tiger Lily: "The Whine-oceris"

I of course, am: "The Tominator"

We waited for the two leggers to retire for the evening before beginning the competition. (better to avoid the possibility of the water squirty thingy)

The first match was a warm-up between Ivan and one of the female two legger's boots that was carelessly left outside its' protective closet. Ivan won handily. He performed a "Sneaky Pete Pounce" and chewed it into submission.

The next match was between Tiger lily and myself. Tiger Lily attempted to stun me with her patented "Whine, Lose or Draw Blood" technique. Fortunately, I countered with a "Paws For Effect" and knocked her flatter than day-old beer.

It was now time for the Main Event.

Ivan and I faced off in the dining room. He poofed his tail in a show of dominance. This cracked me up because it made him look like a traffic cone glued to a basketball. After stifling my inconvenient case of giggles, I laid my ears back and prepared for battle. Turning sideways and crooking my tail, I looked him straight in the eye and said "Bring it on, Tub-a-lump!"

Ivan, unable to control himself, immediately pounced. I absorbed his initial rush by rolling onto my back and adopting the "Nyuk, Nyuk, Nyuk" strategy. This strategy was originally developed by the two legged mixed martial arts team known as "The Three Stooges". It is performed by placing a front paw upon the forehead of ones opponent and utilizing the advantage of longer forelegs to cause your opponent to swing ineffectively.

Ivan eventually realized that he was having no effect and changed his plan of attack. He attempted to use his advantage in sheer mass to pin me and then chomp me at his leisure. This enabled me to exhibit the benefit of being born without bones. Every time he was sure he had me pinned, I would simply "flow" into a different position and bite him in a totally unexpected region of his anatomy.

Finally, Ivan got tired of taking so many bites, and receiving so little nourishment. that he decided to concede. He proceeded to the guest bedroom where he had a romantic evening planned with the big stuffed bunny.

This means that I am the reigning World Wrassling Champion.

This also makes Tiger Lily the reigning World Wrassling Loser.

Unless you count Ivan's big stuffed bunny.

Feline Football League (FFL)

The male two legger is excited. He is happy. He is beside himself with glee. This annoys me. Why is he in such a great mood? Football season begins today. Rah.

Every year the male two legger goes through a mental metamorphosis. Normally he is a mild mannered "live and let live" type, but during football season he suddenly begins to yell at the talking box thingy. He slathers at the mouth and has even been known to kick furniture. While I applaud his new found aggressiveness, after a while it gets tiresome. Therefore, last year I decided to observe this two legged pastime.

I am perplexed. This game seems anathema to all things feline. While the sight of two leggers bashing into each other is somewhat amusing, they are entirely too polite about it. So after much consideration, I have decided to form a feline football league. This will be exactly like the two legger game, but entirely different.

First of all half the two leggers spend their time trying to take the ball thingy away from the other half, only to politely hand it back to them several minutes later. This is not right. In my league, you will get to keep the ball thingy (actually a hamster) until you are either tired of it, or beaten into submission.

Each team will consist of one cat per side and there will be no limit to how many teams can play each game.

Many things that the two leggers consider foul play will actually be encouraged in my league. Smacking, scratching, kicking and biting are to be considered good form.

Points will be awarded on the following basis:

> 6 points for body slamming the team possessing the ball thingy.
> 3 points per poofing
> 3 points per lamp knocked over.

10 points if lamp should break.

3 points for causing the other team to drop the ball thingy.

6 points for killing the ball thingy.

Various points may also be awarded according to the amount of collateral damage inflicted.

No pause between plays. However, if a sunbeam should happen to fall upon the field of play, a mandatory ten minute nap will be taken. Otherwise, play will only be halted for litter box visits or replacement of the old hamster with a fresh, conscious one. The game will end only when one side gives up, the two legger brings out the water squirty thingy, or we run out of hamsters.

Say "Cheesehead"

The Superbowl amuses Ivan.

This year the Superbowl has Ivan positively giddy, as evidenced by the picture above.

You see, Ivan, like my male two legger, is a "Cheesehead".

What is a Cheesehead you ask?

I shall tell you.

From what I have gathered, a Cheesehead is any organism that exhibits any of the following traits:

1. They support the Greenbay Packers Football Team. By support, I of course mean that they eat, live, breath and bleed for the Packers. They will accept someone questioning their ancestry, or insulting their mother, but will instantly turn violent if someone says that the Packers are not the greatest football franchise thingy that ever played the game.
2. They attend football games where the temperature is 200 degrees below zero, completely topless with nothing between them and the elements but green and gold body paint. Though they will don earmuffs if it is snowing.
3. They subsist on a diet of beer, bratwurst, jalapeno poppers and beer on all Sundays between September and February.
4. Their offspring are named Brett, Bart, Aaron or Lombardi.
5. The very thought of a Chicago Bears fan marrying into their family makes them physically ill.
6. They have a sign in their yard that reads "Welcome to Lambeau Field".
7. They have a deep seated belief that anyone that does not support the Packers is either mentally disabled, easily misled, or both. (yet they themselves walk around wearing hats in the shape of a wedge of cheese)

8. They have a shrine to Aaron Rodgers hidden in their closet behind a secret panel that {CENSORED} . . . . nevermind.

There seems to be no geographic limitations to the spread of this mania. Here in the Great Northwest, the Seattle Seahawks are the nearest professional football team, yet everywhere one turns, it is not silver and blue you see, it is green and gold.

Now, on top of everything else, I have been informed that this coming Sunday, I am to host a "Superbowl party thingy". Will the madness ever end? Although truth be told, I am looking forward to the party thingy since I have been informed that several of my online minions will be attending. This will provide an opportunity for much chaos. My two leggers have been manically cleaning and planning for this event. Given that this party is happening Sunday, I plan on spending Saturday night "rearranging".

My house full of Cheeseheads on Superbowl Sunday. It boggles the mind.

Think I'll make Tiger Lily wear a Pittsburgh Steelers sweater.

Everything the Two Leggers
Need to Know They Learned
at a Superbowl Party

As many of you already know, I hosted my first annual Superbowl Party.
I am not a fan of two legger sports.

Ergo, as many of you may already suspect, I had ulterior motives.

I have come to the recent realization that my two leggers are somewhat
lacking in the "Proper manners and courtesies regarding ones four legged
betters" department.

I am not just another devilishly handsome face. Behind these irresistible
eyes lurks a keen and observant brain thingy.

And I HAVE observed.

I have observed that not every two legger walks around their house,
wielding a water squirty thingy like Arnold Schwarzenegger on another
cyborg thingy hunt.

Not every two legger screams and stamps their feet at every broken vase,
shredded curtain or small act of arson. (That brings up a great memory, but
I'll save it for another post)

Not every two legger would lock me in solitary confinement simply
because Tiger Lily donated a little hair and blood to my favorite charity.

In short, my two leggers are in need of some behavioral modification.
According to the talking box thingy, (specifically that Ivan shaped psychiatrist
thingy, Dr. Phil) the best way to change undesirable behavior is to show the
offending two legger proper examples of the desired behavior.

I was aware that every year, football season culminates in a single game
called the Superbowl. On the day of this Superbowl, all two leggers are
required to gather in groups, drink beer, eat fried food and yell maniacally at
the nearest talking box thingy. I do not claim to understand the logic behind
this compulsion, but I did see an opportunity.

I first researched all the two leggers that communicate with my two leggers
via Facebook and e-mail. I made note of all his "friends" that posted cute
pictures of four leggers and joined causes that help less fortunate four leggers.

I then ruled out all those that lived more than four hours away.

This left two prospective "instructors". I convinced my two legger that given my new found popularity, I should host a Superbowl party and submitted my "guest list". My two leggers agreed considering that they have a very large talking box thingy that deserves more than just two-two leggers screaming at it during the Superbowl.

At the appointed hour, Kelly and Shelly arrived at my house and my plan seemed to work perfectly. They immediately commenced to petting and praising me, showering with all the adoration I so richly deserve. They brought me gifts and these unbelievably tasty little treat thingies that were flavored with organic squirrel meat.

They did not yell at me when I sniffed their beer or helped myself to some of their food. The water squirty thingy never even seemed to enter their minds.

I of course rewarded them with much purring and the playful antics that two leggers seem to derive so much joy from.

However, it was to no avail. Every time I hazarded a glance at my male two legger to make sure he was taking notes, he was watching the talking box thingy and yelling. How can he see how good I can be unless he watches?

I finally had to go bite him in order to show him how nice I am.

I am thankful to Kelly and Shelly for their efforts, perhaps we'll try again in the Spring. Until then I may have to simply face the fact:

Some beasts are untrainable.

Hallway Hockey

Last night Ivan and I had a great game of Hallway Hockey. This is truly one of my favorite activities. For those of you unfamiliar with feline sports, perhaps an explanation is in order.

Hallway Hockey has few rules. It basically begins spontaneously with little or no warning. Last nights game began when as I was rearranging some of my two legger's knock knacks, I "accidentally" knocked one off the shelf. This is what is commonly referred to as "putting the puck in play". Ivan immediately took the shot and winged it off the bathroom door. Well played Ivan, well played.

Now the field of play can be described as: anywhere in my house that has a floor hard enough for the puck to travel smoothly and preferably loudly. The only goal is to make as much noise in the middle of the night as we can while simultaneously causing as much collateral damage as possible.

I intercepted Ivan's next shot with my patented "psycho-nut" pounce. This maneuver caused enough noise to wake the male two legger. As he entered the hallway, Ivan and I were prepared. We had already curled together on the couch and were feigning sleep. This left Tiger Lily standing in the hall alone. Though he suspected us, the evidence was against her. Despite her plaintive whining, she was banished to the guest room. Since she took one for the team, I decided not to smack her tonight.

Relocating the puck, I ricocheted a bank shot off the baseboards right at Ivan, who in his zeal for the game, barreled into the trash can knocking it over and spilling its' contents. Incredibly this did not bring about the two leggers. After a few minutes of tense waiting, I decided to resume the game. Alas this was not to be. While I was distracted, Ivan ate the puck.

Mind Game

What once was an occasional hobby, is quickly becoming a competition.

Us felines have decided that the time has come to stimulate the mental health care industry.

We are on a mission to place the two leggers firmly on the path to insanity and paranoia.

Granted, this shouldn't be that difficult to accomplish. (especially where the male two legger is concerned. The road to the nuthouse is but a very short trip for him)

There are rules for this competition:

1. All ideas must be original, or at least non-copyrighted.
2. Insanity must occur within twenty minutes of attempt.
3. Tag teaming is allowed, but not encouraged.
4. Eight leggers may be used, but only in the bathroom.
5. Only three attempts will be allowed in a twenty-four hour period.
6. Extra points will be awarded if the attempt results in the demise of a squirrel thingy.

I began the competition implementing a "spook strategy" by standing in front of a closet, poofing, with my back arched and hissing at the closed door. This resulted in the closet being cleaned the next day.

Ivan, following the same philosophy, ran laps in the hallway in the wee hours. This had the effect of depriving the two leggers of much desired sleep as well as causing several pictures to shake until they hung crooked. This annoyed the female (she cannot abide a crooked picture) but did little to send them over the edge.

Tiger Lily employed a WWMD. (Whiny Weapon of Mental Destruction) She sat on the entertainment center directly in front of the talking box thingy and, you guessed it, whined. This caused the male two legger to:

A. Make unusual faces at her.
B. Say "Sssshhhhhhhh" numerous times.
C. Stamp his feet.
D. Reach for the water squirty thingy before realizing that his prized talking box thingy lay directly in the line of fire.
E. Finally roar at her that he has buried cats before and has no issues with digging another hole.

Those of you who watch the talking box thingy are aware that whenever some two legger grabs a gun thingy and goes out shooting at other two leggers indiscriminately, it is usually soon discovered that all the perpetrators have two things in common:

"They were quiet and kept pretty much to themselves."

And, they had a whiny cat.

I truly thought we had a winner. However, in a raging fit of self control, the male grabbed a beer and calmed himself.

Another stratagem we have been working on is our patented "cat herding chaos" plan. This is a team effort we use as the two leggers are preparing to retire. Each of us runs and hides in separate rooms. The rooms we hide in are, of course, the only rooms we are not allowed to be in while the two leggers sleep. The two leggers are then forced to waste precious sleepy time searching us out and attempting to redistribute us into the rooms in which we are supposed to spend the remaining night time hours.

We have yet to accomplish our goal, but the sudden onset of tremors in the male's hands and the female's newfound facial tic is encouraging.

A Day At The Races

The two leggers screwed up.

They screwed up big-time.

I'm talking a big, big, big and furthermore big mistake.

I am not complaining, not at all. In fact, it made for an amazingly amusing day.

What could they possibly have done to warrant a chapter in my book thingy?

They left a door open, and then left us alone with the open door for nine hours. But the door is not the star of this particular story. It is what lay behind the door that caused the chaos that ensued. They left the door to the cupboard open. Still unaware of the fortuitous nature of their stupidity? Allow me to elaborate:

The cupboard that lies behind this door is none other than the cupboard in which the two leggers store our entire hoard of both food and . . . . wait for it . . . . CATNIP!

Okay, let us pause to consider a moment. We are left alone. We have a 30lb bag of food (conveniently left uncovered). We have a LARGE bag of catnip. And finally, we have a house chock full of knock knacks strewn about the place. What could possibly go wrong?

Of course, the first thing we did was tear into the nip. There was enough for all of us, and even Tiger Lily stopped whining for a while. Then we satisfied our monstrous case of the munchies.

Now came the time to address the Christmas tree.(This occurred during the Holidays) In a very rare instance of tri-feline unity, we all agreed that the tree must be "defoliated". However, it must not be simply attacked, that would be crude and unsophisticated, beneath us. It must be dismantled with malice of forethought. We needed to invent a game in which the tree would become the unfortunate bystander that gets whacked by the flying tire at all NASCAR events.

Contemplating NASCAR, (for my international readers, NASCAR is a sport here in my country where two leggers drive their cars in circles for several hours while being cheered on by other two leggers who are required to be inebriated, wear hats, and live in trailers) I decided a racing game was in order.

At my signal, we ran through my house at top speed. This may sound boring, but given the fact that the floors in my house are made of hardwood and thereby provide little traction, much chaos ensued. Just like in NASCAR, the wrecks provided the most entertainment. Tiger Lily took out the nativity scene in the very first lap, proving that the angel wasn't the only one that could fly. Tiger Lily truly was the straw that broke the camels back.

I wiped out halfway through the third turn on the fifth lap. This sent me sprawling into the packages that had been placed under the tree. Not sure what's in those boxes, but I am fairly certain at least one of them will need some "re-assembly"

Ivan, possibly due to his stubby little legs, seemed to hold the track better than us. Though not as fast as Tiger Lily and I, he still managed a respectable speed in the straight-aways. But on the final lap, Ivan the Lumberingjack lost control. Hitting a slick spot on the track, he flipped end over end and slammed into the trunk of the tree knocking it over and causing it to lean precariously against the wall. Sweet.

Deciding that there was no way we could top this epic exhibition of mindless destruction, I decided a nap was in order.

I awoke several hours later to the sound of the front door opening. I surveyed the room. Broken glass, shattered ornaments and plastic pine needles lay strewn about the living room. Remnants of food wrappings and an empty catnip bag littered the hallway. I was reminded of the talking box thingy when they show the tornado ravaged homes of NASCAR fans.

The gasp of delight that issued from the two leggers when they entered was priceless.

Wad A Wonderful World

I must confess. I have a weakness. Call it a vice, an obsession or even an addiction. I'm not proud of it, I think it weakens me. But I have promised myself to always be completely truthful in this book thingy and therefore would be remiss if I were to hide this basket of dirty laundry. So here goes. I can only hope that you can overlook this shortcoming.

I love wads. There I said it.

Not just any wads. I am as selective in my choice of wads as I am in my hairball thingy placement. The proper wad should be 2-3 inches in diameter. It must be made of either note pad paper or that slightly foily stuff that candy bar wrappers are made of. It must not be so tightly mooshed that it fails to make the proper crackly sound. It can NEVER be made of newspaper as that smacks of recycling and therefore annoys me.

Unfortunately, the manufacture and deployment of wads requires the assistance of a two legger. I have spent much time in the training of my two leggers, teaching them the proper assemblage and launch techniques. The irony being that they honestly believe that they have "trained" me to "fetch". It was a long, incredibly tedious process (two leggers can be dim) but they seem to have finally gained at least a rudimentary understanding of what is expected of them.

The hardest thing to teach them was the proper trajectory of wad flight. The wad should always be thrown so that it forms a perfect parabola of 45 degrees. This allows me time to get under the wad as it begins its' freefall and then bat it out of midair if I so choose. If I choose to allow it to land, the angle enables the wad to skitter across the floor so that I can show off my incredible hockey skills.

After smacking the wad around for several minutes to prove my dominance over all things paper, I then pick it up and return it to the two legged wad launcher and wait for the next round. This can continue for hours.

I have tried several times to introduce my feline minions to the pleasure of the wad, but have thus far failed to stimulate their interest. Tiger Lily just whines about all the smacking involved, and Ivan has a fear of all things round.

There, now you know my dirty little secret. It's out there. Deal with it.

The Curtain Calls

Since the dawn of feline/two legger cohabitation, there has been a point of contention that rises above all others.

Curtains.

Two leggers are driven by instinct to hang vertical panels of cloth over every window they encounter. We feline types are driven to destroy these vertical panels of cloth whenever, and wherever we encounter them. It is the natural order of things.

In every society, on every continent, in every age, there is a two legger hanging curtains and its' feline companion waiting patiently to shred them to bits. This is fact.

There is even a depiction of this painted on the walls of a cave in France. It shows a stone age female two legger hanging a bear skin over a hole in the rock only to find in the morning that a saber toothed tiger had torn it up in the night.

What two leggers fail to understand, is the fact that curtains are like visual catnip. When we enter a room and see all that material stretching from floor to ceiling, we are compelled to act. The feel of our claws piercing the fabric as we propel ourselves ever upward. The sound, like the popping of tiny firecracker thingies, is music to our ears.

We take great pride in our curtain climbing abilities. We even hold competitions.

Ivan has his own peculiar style adapted to his speed to bulk ratio. Though seldom able to climb more than three tailspans vertically, he makes up for this deficiency by often pulling the curtain down to him, rod and all. The chaos and damage this causes more than compensates for the lack of height of climb. His motto: "Attitude Trumps Altitude".

Tiger Lily is de-clawed and therefore disqualified from the competition. Although Ivan and I once convinced her to try anyway. The results were amusing. She ran at the window, leapt with all her might and succeeded in slamming herself bodily into the window screen almost dislodging it in the process. Oh how we laughed.

I prefer technique and artistry in my approach to curtain destruction. My favorite method is to get a running start from the hallway, rounding the corner by ricocheting off the end of the couch, leaping from the floor to the top of the lazyboy, and using the spring of the cushion to launch myself to the very top of the curtain. I then enjoy a relaxing fifteen to twenty second hang time.

The artistry in my method lies in the interesting patterns the sun shining through the holes makes on the carpet. I find them relaxing.

Why do we climb curtains? Because they are there.

Solitary

Much is happening around my house. The two leggers are away most of the time, this being a very hectic time of year for them. Thus, we are left to our own devices in order to keep ourselves amused. While some may see this as a detriment, I see only opportunity.

In the morning before they leave, the two leggers invariably lock me up in one part of my house, and Ivan and Tiger Lily are left in another part of my house. They seem to be under the mistaken belief that this will minimize the damage.

For one thing, I've invented a new game. I call it: "Britches Button Bingo". While the two leggers are absent, I find any pants I can, and chew through the threads that hold the button thingies. How can that be amusing? The key is not chewing completely through the threads, but just mostly through the threads. If this task is performed correctly, the button thingy should not fall off until around 8am when the two leggers are getting ready to leave for the day. Or if you are a true master, the button thingy will fall off later in the day while the two leggers are far from the safe haven of their closet. As always, points are awarded according to the amount of chaos caused.

Ivan spends much of his day glaring at his food bowl. He feels that if he gives it the hairy eyeball long enough, it will magically refill itself out of fear. I have tried many times to explain food bowl physics to him, but once he gets something in his head . . . . well, actually once he gets something in his head, it usually dies of loneliness, but I digress. Let's just say he's stubborn.

Tiger Lily spends most of her day attempting to avoid me. Being locked in a different room, one would think this would be easy, not so. You see, in order to reach the litter box, she must pass by my door. So, I wait. There is a gap between the bottom of the door and the floor. This gap is just large enough that a determined paw can reach out and slap someone. Ivan of course assists in this by standing in the hallway and forcing her to come near the door as she passes.

I'm sure that some of you may see this as mean spirited, however, please be assured, we do this for her own good. I find that a good scare and smacking assists in the litter making process.

iPawed

This morning when my two leggers left my house, I noticed something sitting on my dining room table.

It was the female's computer thingy.

GRIN

We currently have three computer thingies in my house. We have the large one that resides in the room that Tiger Lily is sequestered in at night. It takes up a whole side of the room and is decorated with multiple disks and poorly printed paper thingies. I believe that all these things have been deemed as garbage by the male, but for some inexplicable reason, he ignores the trash bin, preferring to stack all these things around and atop the computer thingy where they can fall while he works causing him much frustration and annoyance. This trash bin remains the cleanest and emptiest of all those within my house. Just another example of confusing two legged behavior.

The second computer thingy is called "The Laptop". This is the computer thingy that I currently write my blog thingy on. In theory, it is supposed to be portable, but it has the curious quality of making the male completely immobile whenever he uses it.

The third and most heavily guarded and highly coveted computer thingy is the one that the male gave to the female for Christmas last year.

She calls it her "iPad". I am confused by the name owing to the fact that it has no eye thingies and it is not soft at all. (I once tried to nap on it and found it too hard to be considered a proper resting place) She takes it with her everywhere she goes and NEVER leaves it unguarded.

Until today . . . .

I found it on the table and decided to attempt to discover what all the hoo-ha was about.

Apparently, it is activated by simply walking on it. I have never witnessed the female stepping on the screen, but it seemed to work for me.

A whole new world opened beneath my blood-stained little paws. (I'll explain the blood-stains some other time, after I come up with a believable alibi) This I-pad thingy has little "icon" thingies all across the screen. Each "icon" triggers what is called an "apt". The term "apt" seems silly because they all seem so useless. There were apts for shooting bird thingies at sheltered pigs, for arranging numbers in big boxes, there was even one that supposedly helps two leggers lose weight.

I soon realized that none of these apt were designed by cats. If I was in charge of designing them, I guarantee there would be differences. The apts I would design are as follows:

1. A screen saver that would show an animated saber tooth tiger gnawing the head of a smurf.
2. Another screen saver that would show an animated saber tooth tiger gnawing the head of a squirrel.
3. Yet another screen saver that would show bunnies playfully hopping through a meadow . . . . until they encounter a saber tooth tiger gnawing the head of a blue squirrel.
4. An apt that would make crashing sounds whenever the two leggers were in the shower.
5. And finally an apt that would create the foulest smelling odor the world has ever known.

Nevermind on that last one. There is already an apt for that.
I have it loaded on my iVan.

Connect the Dots

I received a package in the mail today. (or "the post" for those of you with the really cool accents)

The minion who sent it asked that I keep his/her/it's identity a secret. To say this request caused me some trepidation in opening said package would be a fair statement. Generally, world leaders such as myself do not accept anonymous gifts unless they are stupid, or aspire to martydom. However, I recognized the paw writing and decided to risk it.

After the package was opened, there appeared on my wall a . . . . red dot.

For some unknown reason, one of my minions felt that they could ingratiate themselves to me by sending me a . . . . red dot.

I was not amused.

They could have sent a catnip mousie thingy. They could have sent a feather. They could have sent one of those thingies that make a sound like a two legger farting. They could even have sent me a book on squirrel torture methods and devices. (Illustrated of course)

They sent me a . . . . red dot.

Just as I was about to unleash my utter frustration upon the new pair of shoes that the female two legger brought home yesterday, something happened.

The dot moved.

Not just a little, a LOT. It jumped from wall to wall. It bounced off the ceiling. It skittered across the floor. I felt compelled to kill the dot. Well, perhaps "kill" is too strong a word. Nope, I definitely wanted to kill it. But before killing it, I decided to ponder it.

I sat watching it for a time. Zooming from hither to yon, it soon attracted Ivan's attention. Ivan burst into the room like a wrecking ball wrapped in smelly, striped, orange fur. Knocking over furniture, glassware, lamps and one out of the two resident two leggers, Ivan it seems, felt no love for the red dot either.

The dot disappeared.

It was then that I noticed the male two legger placing a small black cylinder back into the package. Curious, I investigated this object.

It had a button.

I pressed the button.

The dot returned.

I pondered.

That was when it hit me. This was one of those laser thingies.

Oh, the possibilities.

My first thought was that when I see them used on the talking box thingy, stuff usually blows up. This gave me an idea. I waited until Tiger Lily was asleep in the bay window. Carefully, I pointed the laser thingy right at the back of her abnormally large head . . . .

I pushed the button.

To my great dismay, she did not explode. However, she was completely flattened by a wrecking ball wrapped in smelly, striped, orange fur.

This amused me.

Conclusion

Okay, I suppose that I should write something in order to let everyone know that this is the end of this book thingy. I assumed that when the reader turned the last page and saw the back cover, it would be obvious that they had reached the end. However, my two legger informed me that this was not the case and that I should write something in order to avoid confusion.

So in closing, let me just say that this is the end of this book thingy. There are no more words beyond this page. If you happen to discover some words after this page, they are probably written in crayon and were not written by me.

Trust me, this is the last page.

There are no more.

Don't even bother looking.

Just put the book thingy down and walk away.

Why are you still reading?

I said it was over.

THE END

Go away now.

I need a nap.

About The Author

Born and raised in Central Texas, Doug Dunn now lives in Oak Harbor, Washington with his lovely bride and enough animals to provide the cast for a Disney movie. This is the first of what he hopes will be many books to come. He can be contacted by email at: Dougnkatty@yahoo.com

1846337R00119

Made in the USA
San Bernardino, CA
08 February 2013